An African Challenge

This book is Part III of the autobiographical series **An African Life**, including the following titles:

An African Challenge

M. Bettencourt Dias

iUniverse, Inc.
New York Lincoln Shanghai

An African Challenge

iUniverse books may be ordered through booksellers or by contacting:

iUniverse
2021 Pine Lake Road, Suite 100
Lincoln, NE 68512
www.iuniverse.com
1-800-Authors (1-800-288-4677)

ISBN: 0-595-34005-9

Printed in the United States of America

In memory of Dan C. Bettencourt, my son, who loved and understood Africa; and of Christine Caranci Bettencourt Dias, my wife, who came to know it through hardship and sacrifice.

Contents

Acknowledgments

Too many people to mention individually shared their knowledge, advice, and encouragement during the preparation of this book and the others in this series. I especially want to thank Michelle de la Rosa, Cristina V. Grilo and Paulo H. Botinas for help with the manuscript; Fred M. Siebolds and Julie Kinder for help with the publication; Margaret Kinder for editing assistance; John Kinsey, Carlos G. Alves, Danilo S. Picolo, and my sisters Céu and Lily, for the use of their photographs; Maria J. Rolão for the loan of the maps of Mozambique; Kristi R. Jue for technical assistance with the illustrations and the design of the book; Dr. Artur F. Nunes and my cousin João Dias Afonso for research which I used to a great extent…and my wife Christine for the incentive to start writing.

To all, my deepest gratitude and thanks.

Introduction

This is the third book of a series that started with *An African Name* and was followed by *An African Career*. In the three books, I attempt to guide the reader through a period in the history of the Dark Continent that is mostly untold. My intention is to link the progress of Angola and Mozambique, two large Portuguese colonies located on opposite sides of the African Continent, to my own personal experience from my early teens in Angola and as I grew to manhood in Mozambique. The pace of change was very quick, and in less than a person's lifetime these two colonies became relatively modern, efficiently governed countries—especially when compared to many of the surrounding countries.

I went to Mozambique with my parents in 1934 and entered the only high school then in existence, in a country that is 302,000 square miles in area and extends along the western shore of the Indian Ocean for a distance of 1,760 miles. It was during the time I lived there that towns, ports, railways, airfields, hospitals, schools and one university were built and began to operate with high standards of efficiency.

My parents were schoolteachers who had emigrated from the Azores Islands, first to Angola and from there to Mozambique. As soon as they arrived in Mozambique, the Education Department sent them to the most remote areas in order to pioneer education of the African tribes. The first step was getting there, and that was no mean feat. They had to sail along the east coast of Africa in tiny vessels, disembark at tiny ports, and travel into the interior on trucks or at the head of a line of porters. Then they would establish a "permanent" Center of Operations, become friends with the chiefs of the local African tribes, and convince them that their children needed to be educated. They would stay until the schools were built, while simultaneously training the future local teachers. I had grown up in this pioneering environment.

After one year of high school in Lourenço Marques,[1] I returned to the bush and continued studying at home under my father's guidance. My parents had not been able to afford the continuing expense of my boarding, or the many other costs (travel, school fees, supplies) associated with my attendance at the high school. Eventually, my parents were transferred to a place near the border with Swaziland, and I learned English from Scottish missionaries. From there I went to South Africa, entered a mining school, and after a year started working underground in a deep gold mine.

I returned to Mozambique in 1943 and joined the Geological Survey as a translator. A few years later, I was awarded a scholarship to study in an American mining school. I entered the Colorado School of Mines, and graduated with a Master's degree in Mining Geology in 1951. That same year I married Christine, a resident of Denver, Colorado who was studying for an advanced degree at Denver University. We traveled back to Mozambique in a cargo ship, and I rejoined the Geological Survey. During my career there, I took part in most of the expeditions that systematically studied the geology of the country, opened up roads, and built bridges that made possible the development of the mining industry from its very start.

The idea of writing the three books came to me on a stormy evening in 1975, in the beautiful city of Colorado Springs, Colorado. At the time, I was a penniless immigrant; my family had been forced to leave Mozambique and to leave behind everything we had saved. We had fled after the takeover of the Portuguese African colonies by guerillas, orchestrated by Communist factions and led by Russian-trained thugs. I was trying to hitch a ride home during a snowstorm, when two women stopped their car and let me in. They probably noticed the thin clothing I wore in the middle of a Colorado blizzard, and asked what country I was from. I replied that I came from Mozambique, and they roared with laughter. When the merriment stopped they apologized, and one explained that they owned the car in partnership and one of the rules was that they would not pick up hitchhikers unless they came from some truly remote place such as Mozambique—a country they did not know the location of, but which had such a romantic-sounding name! I knew that someday I wanted to commit my experiences to paper.

Naturally, I was kept quite busy for several years afterwards as we tried to rebuild the family's finances up to a safe level. Meanwhile the book project rested in a deep drawer labeled "Projects to be picked up again when I have time." And there it stayed until I retired and Christine and I came to live in Portugal in 1986. After we settled down, Christine got after me to start writing.

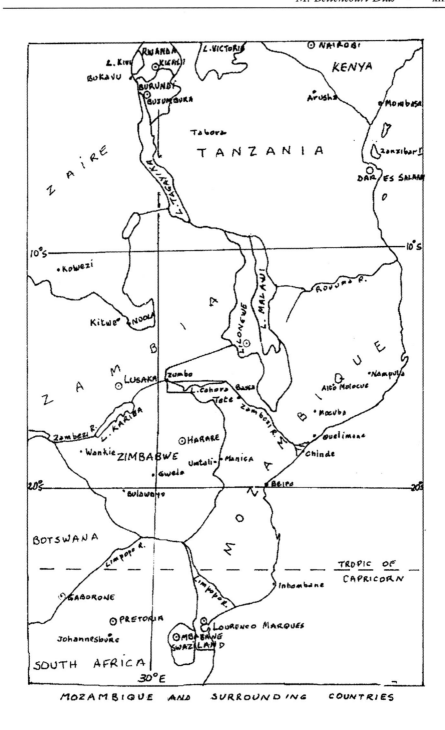

MOZAMBIQUE AND SURROUNDING COUNTRIES

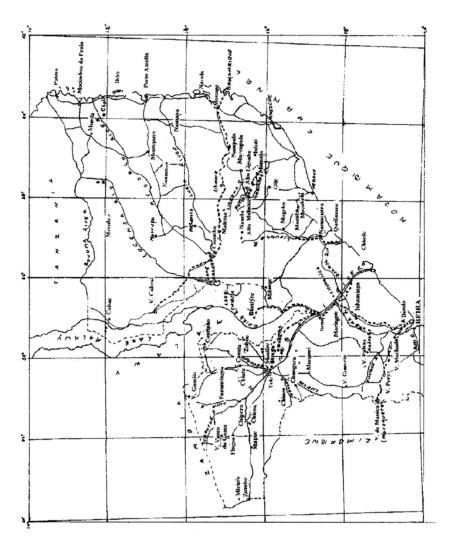

Northern Mozambique, showing principal towns, rivers, and railroads.

CHAPTER ONE

Out of the Door

I was obligated to work for the Geological Survey of Mozambique during seven years, to repay the government scholarship that enabled me to attend the Colorado School of Mines.[2] I had the good fortune during my first years of working under Alexandre Borges, who advanced from chief geologist to director during my tenure. But after his death, my relationship with his replacement became more and more strained. I had been in the field doing a seven-month field study of the unique geology inside the crater of the extinct Muambe volcano. After I returned to the head office and the immediate presence of the new director, appointed by the Government of Portugal, I decided I would leave the Survey as soon as my contract ended.

By late 1956, I had only about four months remaining in my contract and no prospects for another job in sight. Unexpectedly, a company I had never heard of applied for an Exclusive Prospecting License to an area of 3,000 square kilometers (nearly the area of the state of Rhode Island). Exclusive Permits to prospect for minerals over large areas of the territory were allowed by the mining laws, provided the applicant produced proof of having the professional and financial resources needed to carry out the task.

Although Mozambique had been promoted from the previous rank of "Colony" to that of "State," the central government in Lisbon still did not allow us to decide about such requests without their authorization. It was my job to write a detailed paper about the geography, natural resources, population, accessibility, means of communication, geology and mineralization of the area, as well as a history of the past successes and business failures of the applicant. Based on the data we supplied (and more often on the political strings that were pulled by the applicants in Lisbon), permission might be given to explore and to register in their name any mineral deposits found.

I drew up a map showing the area in question, outlined in a bright color. I wrote that there were no roads in the area and the Geological Survey had never done any work there. I noted that it was coursed by three large rivers and numberless tributaries; that it was believed to be covered by forests; that (according to information from the Tsetse Fly Control Commission) it harbored tsetse flies; and that about one-fifth of the 1,350 square miles under consideration were inside a game reserve. Here I played dumb, and supplied another map showing the overlap of the two areas. I went on to explain that the purpose of game reserves was to protect the animals from having contact with obnoxious humans, of which prospectors were good examples.

The rest of the report was even easier. I stated that I had never heard of the mining company in question, which precluded me from having to pass judgment on their character and finances. As for the geology of the area, I repeated that it had never been studied by the Survey, but that we believed it was "made up mostly of metamorphic rocks." This was a very useful expression, especially adapted to describing areas about which you knew nothing.

Just to show that I took the request very seriously, I ended my dissertation by saying, "should the Lisbon Authorities, with their superior knowledge, be in agreement, I humbly suggest that the area inside the game reserve should not be included in the exclusive permit, but that an equivalent area could be given elsewhere." And, I added another map showing two alternative areas that the Lisbon bureaucrats could choose from, and then take credit for such a "brilliant" solution!

The director read my "masterpiece" and asked whether we could not give more geological information. I answered, "Certainly. We can send in an expedition as soon as the rainy season ends. In a few months we should be able to tell Lisbon which areas are gneisses and which are schists."

"No, leave it as is," he replied. "I doubt whether the interested party would pay the costs of the expedition, and Lisbon, for certain, will not."

I assumed that an unknown mining outfit with no experience in geological exploration would have second thoughts about the project when Lisbon showed them what I had to say, and I promptly forgot about the matter. Moreover, I was handling the lion's share of the daily load of problems running a large organization because the director concentrated only on projects that got his name mentioned in the press. So I waded into the bureaucratic swamp and slogged through that morass, as much as I hated it.

Two months later, my secretary came in to say that there was a person wanting to talk to me. The visitor insisted that it had to be today because he was flying to

Quelimane early in the morrow. She had given the man a picture, painted in somber colors, of the state in which I was overworked and overloaded with commitments, but it had been a wasted effort as the man had not budged. She was of the opinion that it might be a good idea to talk to him and get it over with. I agreed with the wisdom of her suggestion. She brought in a very large man on whose card I recognized the name that had signed the application for the Exclusive Prospecting Permit which I had processed. Assuming that he had come for news of his request, I told him that it had been sent to Lisbon, accompanied by all the documentation necessary, "about two months ago."

"That is not the purpose of this visit," he said. "The Permit has already been issued to us. I expected that you knew. Your director has been informed. What brings me here today is that one of the clauses in the contract specifies we must place in charge of the operations a person whose professional competence is recognized by the Lisbon authorities. However, all the geologists and engineers who answered our ads in the press, and whose names we submitted to the Lisbon authorities, were turned down."

I wrote down on a piece of paper the names of three men who had previously worked for the Survey, and handed over the list to him. After reading it, he shook his head. "The first one on this list is out of the country," he said. "The second is not interested in our offer, and the third one, we do not want him." He paused, looked straight in my eyes and, pronouncing his words slowly, continued: "There is one name that everybody finds acceptable. And that is why I am here. We would like to have you be our director of operations."

The words caught me completely off-guard. While I stared at him, my mind tried to react and cope with the unexpected; he got up, handed me another card, and said, "I know my offer comes as a surprise. I also know how busy you are (you have a very loyal, and very convincing, secretary). I have a few things to take care of before I return to Quelimane on the early flight tomorrow. I ask you to please think about our offer and let us know at this address. The area for which we requested an exclusive prospecting permit is a very interesting one, known to very few people, and I am sure you will love it. Goodbye."

After the man left, my first reaction was to get more information about him and his company. I called an old friend, the owner of a long-established business who knew most of the important businessmen in the country. From him I learned that my caller had started as a young immigrant from Portugal. He had made his first money during the construction of the railway from Quelimane to Mocuba, and had re-invested it in modern, efficient cotton mills that had been very successful in the Zambezi District. He had then branched into tea processing and was now pouring capital into the tea plantations, themselves. According to my friend, the man was a hard worker and expected a lot from his associates, but was known to be a fair and generous employer.

As soon as I got home that evening, I told Chris of the unexpected visitor and of his proposal. "It seems like the answer to our prayers," she said. "What will the salary be?"

"Neither salary nor any other details were discussed," I replied. "He was in a hurry but was quite frank in admitting that they are in a bind to find a director of operations who can fulfill the conditions set in their contract. Without a director of operations acceptable to the Lisbon big wheels, he will not be given the green light to start operations. Which means that I can pretty much ask whatever I want, within reason of course."

"What worries me is that, according to the information from our friend, they have no experience in mining. Their background is in cotton, tea, timber, and trading. He and I seem to belong to completely different worlds. I need a lot more information about this man and his companies before considering the cons of the offer. The pro is the likelihood of a good salary."

"How about your father?" Chris asked. "Did he not pioneer education in the Zambezi Valley? He probably knows all about the man. Why don't you call him?"

Over the phone, Dad said he did not know the man personally. "But, I have heard a lot about him. He is a legend. Built a small empire based on cotton and timber, but curiously, it seems he did it through hard work because I never heard his name tied to any scandals. Never heard that he was into mining, either. Where is this mining concession located?"

When I described the area to him, Dad said, "That is smack in the middle of unexplored Africa! I have never been near it, don't know anybody who has, and, if I remember rightly, the last time anybody crossed it from north to south, it was the German Army during the First World War! I'll ask around and call you when I pick up more information."

When I got home the next evening, Chris showed me the draft of a contract that she had composed and typed. It specified a salary that was nearly three times what I was making at the Survey, included rent-free furnished housing, company car and gas, a generous expense account, one month's vacation with full pay each year, free transportation to the capital every twelve months, a six-month vacation on full pay every four years, and free medical care and full insurance coverage for every member of the family.

After reading it carefully I said, "At least this will give us a basis from which to bargain, and it clearly conveys the idea that geological talent does not come cheap. I like it. Let's type it in a final format and mail it, before we get cold feet."

In those days, telephone connections between towns in Mozambique were still very unreliable, and everything was handled by letter or by telegram. I did not expect a counter offer to arrive for at least a month, did not tell anybody outside the family about the prospective job, and continued with my normal routine at the Survey.

Relations between myself and the director became even more strained when we were informed by the Governor General's office that there was going to be a budget surplus and that nearly $70,000 of it might come to us for scientific equipment. I had systematically—and unsuccessfully—requested new equipment in every report from the Survey, during the period that I was acting director after Borges' death and until the new director was appointed.

I was handed a folder containing information about a French metallurgical testing laboratory existing at the Mines Department of Tananarive, Madagascar, which the director had picked up during one of his visits to the Island. The facility was for the treatment of graphite and was hardly adaptable to our more eclectic needs.

After studying it, I told him that we badly needed up-to-date petrographic equipment and an assay laboratory, not a plant specialized in the treatment of graphite. He insisted that I translate the materials into Portuguese and write a proposal justifying the need for building a similar facility.

When I pointed out that such a facility would cost more than the sum that had been promised, he said, "That is just fine. After we get the money we will say that it is not enough for what we need, and then we will use it for other things."

I realized that what he was planning was to have me sign the proposal, so that I could be blamed later for whatever happened to the funds that would be made available through the Governor General's efforts. To avoid more arguments, I returned the folder to him with a note saying that my French was not adequate, and that, since he spoke French fluently, he could handle the subject himself to better advantage.

The next day I received a note from the chief of personnel. The note informed me that I had been placed under "disciplinary procedure, for having refused to obey an explicit order from my direct superior." Furthermore the note said that I would be called upon to answer a bill of accusations, and that I would not be allowed to leave town without the director's permission!

When I got home that evening, and before I had a chance to tell Chris how I had been put in the "dog house" at work, she handed me a telegram that had arrived a couple of hours earlier. It read: "YOUR TERMS FOR POSITION DIRECTOR OF OPERATIONS ARE ACCEPTED STOP WHEN CAN YOU START QUESTION SELF ARRIVING POLANA HOTEL MONDAY STOP PLEASE CONTACT STOP MONTEMINAS."

"Wonderful!" said Chris. "Let's call Grandma Dias to see if she can take Danny while we go out and celebrate! Who is this Monteminas?"

"I am told that the names of all the companies owned by my prospective employer start with the prefix Monte. 'Monteminas, Ltd.' is the mining company."

When I went to meet him at the Polana Hotel, I said that I could start working in about a month's time, but that I did not know whether the fact that I was under "disciplinary procedure" had any effect on my resigning from the Survey. I informed him further that I had made an appointment with a lawyer to discuss the subject and would be seeing him in a couple of days.

He asked me to go over what had happened in detail, after which he phoned his lawyer, repeated what I had said, and asked, "What is the best way for him to leave the Survey in the shortest time, and with the least amount of trouble?"

After listening to the lawyer for a while, he hung up and said, "Your director has no right to restrict your movements and needs to be put in his place. Tomorrow morning, go to the chief of personnel of the Survey, and hand him a written request to be present at the next meeting of the Government Medical Board. You do not have to tell him why you want to go before the medical board. It is not his business. He just has to get you the appointment.

"Tell the doctors that you work extra hours every week and that you feel tired and nervous. Do not mention the strained relations with the director, but if they ask any questions, answer them openly. What you tell the doctors is privileged information that cannot be supplied to the director under any circumstances. They will probably give you a month to rest and recuperate. Your contract will be up at the end of the month. Our lawyer will prepare all the paperwork for your resignation and will file it with the Survey. He thinks your director will have second thoughts about the disciplinary action, when he finds out you have a good lawyer behind you."

The next day, I requested that the personnel manager get me an appointment with the Medical Board. I was told later that the doctors would see me in one week, at the next meeting.

When I walked into the meeting room of the Medical Board, I saw a long table behind which sat five serious-looking gentlemen wearing three-piece suits. I assumed they were the doctors, who were prepared to ask me embarrassing questions about the state of my health. In front of the long table, there was one lone chair. The doctor sitting in the middle of the long table looked at me and said, pointing in the direction of the chair, "Please be seated. Are you Manuel Bettencourt Dias, a geological engineer employed by the Geological Survey?"

I replied, "Yes sir, I am."

Turning to one of the other doctors, he said, "Would you please conduct the examination?"

The man nodded, turned his head to me, and said, "Do you still work as hard as you did when we last met inside a volcano in Benga?"

It was only then that I recognized him. He had accompanied Dr. Xavier de Basto, head of the Sleeping Sickness Mission, on a visit to my geological group to check on our health. At the time, I was in charge of the investigation inside the crater of the volcano called Mount Muambe.

"I apologize for not recognizing you, Doctor Ferreira. The work here in the city is different, but the hours are long and the responsibility is heavy on my shoulders. I am worn out."

He turned to the other doctors and said, "This is one geologist I have seen at work in the field. When he says he is tired, I have no doubt it is so. I would like to recommend to the Board a period of rest of sixty days to recuperate from asthenia caused by overwork." The other doctors nodded their heads.

The presiding doctor addressed me saying, "You may go. You are on vacation for sixty days starting tomorrow. Have a good rest. Please hand this signed order to your personnel officer."

On my return to the office, I packed all my personal papers and settled all pending matters with the help of my astonished secretary. I had a meeting with the draftsman and instructed him on how to finish the geological maps he was working on. Then, a few minutes before closing time, I went to the personnel officer and handed him the order of the Medical Board.

"Sixty days?!" he exclaimed, "How did you manage that? You don't even look sick! What did the director say when you told him?"

"He did not say anything because I did not tell him anything. You tell him. Goodbye!"

I never saw the director again. Monteminas' lawyer handled the paper work involved in my formal resignation, when the seven years of my contract were up.

Then, while I concentrated on devising a plan of operations to prospect the concession area that had been awarded to Monteminas, Ltd., Chris got herself and baby Dan ready to travel to Colorado. They would stay with her parents until such time as I managed to create adequate conditions for them to stay with me in the middle of Unknown Africa.

A few days after they left for Colorado, I flew to Quelimane. I took with me the operational plans I had prepared, as well as all the maps and necessary geological field equipment that could be purchased in Lourenço Marques.

At the headquarters of Monteminas I was given all the information (not much and rather vague in nature) that had been assembled from talking to elephant hunters and traders who were the only people who had traveled in the area where the concession was located.

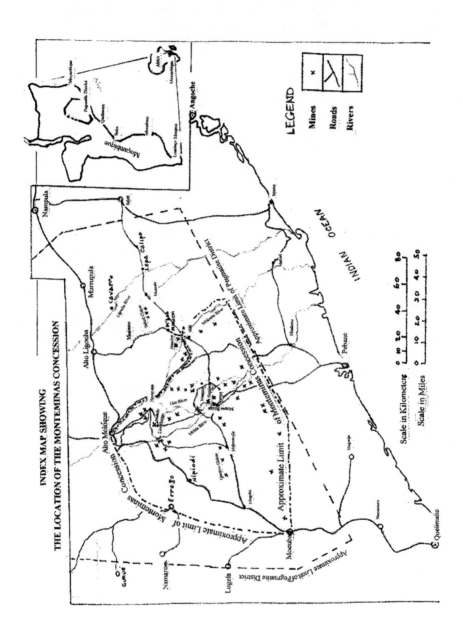

The most important fact I found while reading what the local personnel had gathered, was that a road connecting the county seat of Alto Molócuè to an administrative post named Gilé ran along the high ground between the valleys of the Molócuè and Melela Rivers and was maintained open during most of the year.[3] It seemed to be the closest access to the northern part of the concession, because that divide was also the northern limit of the "exclusive prospecting area" of Monteminas. I decided to try entering the concession area from that end.

After one week of preparation in the city of Quelimane, the expedition got on the road at the beginning of the second quarter of 1957. The convoy included a five-ton truck carrying camping equipment, food supplies, tools, and fuel drums; and a pick-up truck with medical supplies, laboratory and other scientific equipment, battery-powered radio communications equipment (which in those days was still bulky, heavy and unreliable), and personal baggage.

I had requested that the company give me a four-wheel-drive personal vehicle, so that I could move around using bush trails made by hunters and traders. But my employer suggested that it would be far more comfortable to drive a Volkswagen "Beetle." When I showed surprise at the suggestion, he told me that during his trips to inspect cotton farms spread all over Zambezia he had found a Volkswagen to be the most reliable and comfortable means of transportation. Therefore, I decided to give it a try and led the column of vehicles driving a brand-new black Beetle. We made it to Alto Molócuè at the end of the first day and spent the night at a small hotel.

The next morning I paid a visit to the office of the Mines Department, which was headed by an old friend. From him I gathered all the available information about the area. In condensed form, it said that the area could be described as "almost totally unexplored; some rare minerals were known to have come out of it; the natives panned for gold in some rivers that only they knew of; all of the area was covered with forest; and no roads existed."

He suggested checking out an old African road that followed the high ground between the courses of the Melela and the Lice Rivers.[4] According to his information, this now-abandoned track had in years past been of strategic importance. During the First World War, it had been used alternately by the German Army and by our side.

"You might repair it for use by vehicles and thus have access to the central part of your concession. I cannot give you more detailed information because I have never had reason to go into that region. Very few people have visited those wilds. The best way to find where the African road is located will be to stop at Novanana and ask the chief. He is a nice guy: Paramount Chief of the Achirima, no less, but a very helpful old person. I suggest that you take a small gift *to show your respect.* Small gestures like that have a lot of meaning for Africans. It will convey to him that you are aware of their customs; that you appreciate his social position is such that he is entitled to receive gifts; but that you, as well, have a social position high enough that you do not have to give valuable gifts.

"It is difficult to find laborers out that way, and a good word from the chief to his subjects will be extremely valuable. I will write him a note introducing you as my friend. In the note I will mention that you are going to work in the area of his chiefdom, looking for minerals.

"But I will also inform him that you are working for a private company, so as to avoid suggestions of any connection between us besides personal friendship."

CHAPTER TWO

Into the Unknown

Our survey team consisted of the surveyor, who had previously worked with me inside the Muambe volcano, and an African driver from Quelimane. That night we slept at Chief Novanana's village in a brand new bamboo and grass guest-hut, to which the chief personally conducted us.

The hut had two bedrooms, a dining room, and an ample porch. At the back there was a bathroom with a water bucket, from which you could pour water over yourself using an enamel cup. Next door there was a "hole-in-the-ground" toilet. Everything was spotlessly clean.

After a *makua* shower,[5] I went to the chief's *Ondaba* Hut where business matters were conducted. I explained to him that we were going to look for minerals. In the process we would cut new roads, repair old ones, and build camps and bridges. We would need lots of workers, would pay them good wages, and would give them good clothes and blankets. We had medicines to treat common illnesses and would treat any of his people who came to our camp for help. I handed him the letter from the Mines Department man. He read it, asked how his friend was, and inquired what he could do for us.

When I mentioned the old African road he said, "Yes, it is very old. When the Portuguese came to make war against the slavers of the Parapato, they used it to build the fort at Morrua. From there it goes west to Mulevala and south to Mualama. When I was a young man, there was war with German Tanganyika. The German army entered this area. The tribes here took the side of the Portuguese. I fight also. Much of the fighting took place along that old road. Tomorrow I will show you where it crosses this road," he said, pointing to where our cars were parked. "Then we will follow it until it comes to the Lice River. There we stop. Cars cannot cross the Lice. There is no bridge."

The next morning he came with me in the Beetle and the others followed until he asked me to stop. We got out and he pointed to a track that was almost invisible on the right side of the road.

"That is the old road to Morrua. It was a footpath that the military widened. But a good many years have been by since; the bridges were allowed to fall down, and no cars have used it. You go slow, so that the other cars can follow."

I turned into the abandoned track with the trucks following behind me, and we slowly advanced towards the valley of the Lice River. There were bushes growing all over, and we had to stop many times to cut them and to remove windfalls. After about ten kilometers of slow progress, we reached an open area with a view of the river flowing peacefully below a long hill.

"This good place for camp," said Chief Novanana. "No big trees to cut. Wind carries away the mosquitoes. Water not too far away. Lice River never goes dry. If you like the place, tomorrow I can send some men to help you build camp."

The other vehicles arrived and, after making a quick reconnaissance, I told them where they could set up the tents while I drove the chief back to his village.

During the trip, I inquired about the labor situation.

"From villages surrounding mine, I think it will be possible to find about five dozen men. I talk to some of them today. They show up tomorrow at your camp. I will send runners to other villages that are further away. Maybe about as many men will come in a few days."

I thanked him for his help, and asked if he knew anybody who could cook. He smiled and said, "Now that is a very difficult wish to fulfill here in the bush. But you are very lucky person, I think, because a man who used to cook for some white people in Mocuba has been home for a while and needs a new job. His house is along this road. We can stop there for you to talk to him."

When I returned to our new camp, I brought with me the most difficult specialist to find in the bush: a cook!

The surveyor had directed the unloading of camping items and parked the vehicles in a grass-free area where they would be safe from bush fires. He was assisting the driver in removing grass and bushes from the area where the tents would be erected. I picked up a *panga*[6] and gave another to the new cook. We joined the cleaning brigade and set to work establishing the clearing, which would prevent wild fires from progressing through camp and discourage small animals and insects from crossing it.

A couple of hours later, two local men appeared armed with their spears and bush knives. They "had heard the cars, and had come to see if they could help." This was said in the melodious twang of the Achirima language with smiles and respectful bows.

I thanked them, and said that we would appreciate it if they went to get some water from the river. They clapped their hands saying, "How come you speak our language?"

"Well," I said, "I do not speak it too well but I learned it at Alto Ligonha. You please go and fill these canvas bags with water and bring them back."

I gave them four canvas water bags. They held them suspiciously in their hands. Then they saw the cook, whom they evidently knew, and explained to him that if you carried water inside a piece of cloth you would be *"metehko de mahala"* (working for free). Bags were for corn, not for water. I told the cook, who spoke fluent Portuguese, to go with them and choose a place where the water was clean. There, they would learn that these bags could carry water after they had been soaked for a few minutes.

Before it got dark we had the tents erected, and the cook had a hot meal cooking over sets of three stones with burning sticks between them, in the centuries-old African way.[7] I paid the two tribesmen who had come to help us and gave them some salt. I added that if they wanted to come and work regularly they would be welcome. They later became the veterans of our work force.

This photo of the original Alto Ligonha forest was taken in 1955, before I left the Survey. Even as I arrived to work in the Monteminas concession, the precious hardwood trees were being cut and the forest was giving way to subsistence farming. Today, the original forest is completely gone. The tall grass seen on the left would stay soaked with the night's dew until mid-morning. Geologists and workers who moved about in the morning would be soaked to the skin until the sun dried the grass. Photo by the author.

CHAPTER THREE

A School in the Jungle

During the following week, we concentrated on making the camp functional. While the surveyor was building the usual bamboo huts with grass roofs for an office, a dining room, a kitchen, a radio-shack, toilets, vehicle maintenance shop, blacksmith's workshop, and warehouses, I selected a car assistant.[8] Capitalizing on his knowledge of the geography, we piloted the Beetle through various and sundry jungle tracks that led to various and sundry villages where he introduced me to the local notables. I had long talks with them explaining what we were doing, and we started to forge good social relations.

Naturally, because neither can a leopard change the spots on its hide, nor can a geologist keep his hands off rocks, I also stopped to pay my respects to various and sundry rock families. I also stopped every time I had a good view of the countryside from the top of some hill, to study in much detail all the landmarks that were the only beacons available for orientation.

This end of the concession was covered with a mixed forest of tall trees. Among the many different species, *Brachistegia spiciformis* was predominant. The trees grew spaced enough apart from each other to allow abundant light penetration. As a result, the ground was covered with grasses and bushes of many kinds and some were in bloom. Orchids grew, attached to the trunks of trees in places where they were protected from direct exposure to sunlight. There were several kinds of palms, and in the glades, the grass grew taller than a man. Creepers formed patches of impenetrable jungle on the banks of the streams.

In this region the rains fall in one season only: from November to April. The weather during the months without rain, considered the long East African winter, is characterized by very pleasant nights, while the days are warm and sunny but never too hot. Heavy dew falls during the night and soaks the grass and the bushes. It maintains the soil just moist enough to keep the plants alive during the half of the year during which it does not rain. The dew was also created for the purpose of reminding geologists that all earthly paradises have, when you get down to know them intimately, some serious flaw. In this case, the morning dew forces you to either wait until about ten in the morning to start your field work (thus wasting half of the morning), or get used to being thoroughly soaked and shivering with cold for a few hours every day.

In the same way that every fruit-bearing tree growing in the forest is claimed by some village (where you have to go and ask permission to harvest the fruit), most places suitable for camping, for farming, or for installing a village, have names. The place where we camped was called Malolo, and therefore we gave the same name to the camp.

During our second week at Malolo, two big-game hunters and three "prospectors" hired by our headquarters reported for work. Four young men from the cotton-growing division of the mother company and three ex-soldiers who had just finished their military service also arrived to complete the field staff.

I interviewed them individually and concluded that most had very little education. The professional hunters were at home in the jungle, but that was all. The young cotton buyers had never stepped into the bush. The soldiers had been trained by the army to survive in the jungle, and now they seemed eager to learn how to become prospectors.

In view of the fact that this was the clay from which I had to mold the future members of a prospecting crew, there was only one thing to do: put all of them through an intensive training program. The students would have to learn the basics of orientation in an environment where, although there was no thick vegetation completely surrounding them all of the time, it was difficult to observe the horizon. They would have to learn how to move around without getting themselves eaten by wild animals; how to avoid tropical diseases; and how to apply basic notions of physical geology, mineralogy and petrology. They would also have to acquire the ability to describe in writing what they saw in the field.

By this time we had our radio unit in operation, and I was able to talk (when atmospheric conditions allowed) with the president of Monteminas, who was more than 400 kilometers away in Quelimane. To make life "easier" for us, the Post Office Department of the Government did not permit private citizens to talk "business" over their radios. The government monitored transmissions, and imposed heavy fines on anyone caught talking "business." These stupid restrictions forced us to talk at five o'clock in the morning, under the assumption that the P.O. monitors were not paid enough to encourage them to be up that early. A very clever code was also invented in which plain, innocent words and names had specific different meanings, adapted to our needs.

I could contact headquarters with a battery fed transmitter. I had also a little marvel of engineering which ran on gasoline and kept the battery charged. As soon as I realized that the men had to be put through an intensive training program, I informed my employer. *"I have organized a soccer team but my players need intensive coaching before they can play with confidence. I suggest that your team be patient until my players become more proficient. They are very keen and taking their education seriously."*

Thus was the "Malolo University" born. The students were "housed" two to each canvas tent. The "professors" (the surveyor and I) had individual tents. In the center of the camp there was a hut for the classroom, which doubled as the dining room and after-hours lounge; a laboratory where the students practiced and learned physical and chemical tests to identify minerals; and the kitchen.

The campus of the "Malolo University." At left are two canvas tents which were part of the students' dormitory. In the center, set amongst the trees, are the classroom and laboratory. The kitchen and warehouses are at the far right, spread apart to minimize fire hazard. Photo by the author.

Reveille was at sunrise. Each morning, a different student took a hammer to a steel bar that hung on a rope from the branch of a tree. This caused a din that was very effective at making everyone in camp wide-awake, and was also heard in the workers' camp located on the banks of the Lice River, downstream from our camp. The same student took the daily roll call, and assigned tasks to the hired African personnel. These tasks included keeping our camp swept clean and supplied with water, the chickens fed, and the kitchen supplied with firewood. Each week, the menu and the responsibility of running the cooking staff fell on a different person. Some "hotel managers" showed traces of aptitude for the job, but most were a total disaster.

The first class of the day started at 7:30 a.m. I taught all subjects dealing with geology, mineralogy, and prospecting practice. The surveyor taught the students how to read maps, how to keep themselves from getting lost, and how to register and describe whatever they would find out there. Classes ended about noon. Students and teachers had lunch together, followed by an hour's rest period. Then the students piled into the pickup and were driven to points chosen by the surveyor, where they were divided into groups of three. They were issued maps showing the point where the pickup had dropped them off, a few notable reference points, and the point where the pickup would be waiting to recover them at the end of the exercise. Usually they had to walk through the jungle for about five kilometers to reach the rendezvous. The men with bush experience served to rescue lost groups.

If a party failed to reach the waiting pickup after it got dark, a rescue group would be sent to help them. Firstly, the rescuers would fire into the air three rifle shots in quick succession.[9] Then they would listen for a similar answer that would tell them the direction in which the lost party was located.

At the end of the first month, I started to go out with the students once a week for exercises that lasted the whole day. We drove out to a point chosen by me. One man was given the map and a compass; another carried the rifle. Food, water and field equipment were distributed among the others. The group advanced in a wide front, with the men positioned about twenty meters apart, and the "navigator" and me in the center. I would give a bearing to the "navigator," and we would start to walk in that direction. Every student was supposed to observe the rocks in his path with care. If anyone met with rocks that he did not recognize or saw signs of mineralization, he would whistle to call all the others to go to see it. I classified the rocks and explained whatever they meant, and then we took up the march again. I changed the bearing gradually so as to get back to the camp at the end of the day.

During the first exercise as we neared the Malolo camp, one of the men called the group to see what he had found. The man, named Zacarias, had worked in a gold mine in Portugal. When I got to him, I saw that he had found the outcrop of a pegmatite.[10] Everyone was all excited, and had chunks of quartz, feldspar, and mica in their hands. They were all talking at the same time, and wanting to know if their classifications were correct. I had them sit around me and talked to them about pegmatites.

We got back to camp about shower time, which was at dusk. The excitement among the men about their discovery of some of the minerals I had been telling them about in the classroom gave me the first indication that I had succeeded, to some extent, in infecting them with the prospecting bug. That evening after dinner, I asked everyone to write on a piece of paper the name that each thought should be given to the first discovered pegmatite. Most of them suggested Malolo Pegmatite, and it was thus christened.

Next I told them to think about how one should proceed to learn whether it was economically mineralized, because the next morning they would be given two hours in the classroom to present their plans for developing it.

The most complete plan of studying the pegmatite in detail was presented by Zacarias, the man who had discovered it. He proposed sinking a series of prospecting pits about one meter deep, located on a rectangular grid, and spaced twenty meters apart along the length of the outcrop. The contents of each pit would be examined for valuable minerals, and the fines would be panned. I was impressed and asked him to explain to the group why he thought this would show whether the pegmatite was economically mineralized, or not. He backed his plan quite adequately.

"I agree with this method," I said. "Starting tomorrow, Mr. Zacarias can choose ten men from our workers. They will work under his direction for two weeks. At the end of two weeks, I will evaluate the work done. Then the other students will have their turn at being in charge of the program."

During the first week, one of the prospecting pits produced a few kilos of commercial beryl. In the second week, more beryl was found in other pits and the panning of fines showed concentrates of tantalite. In view of the results, the number of workers sinking pits was doubled.

Eventually, everybody did two weeks in charge of pit-sinking, in order to learn what a prospecting program involved and to get the feel of leading a crew of African laborers.

In the mean time, the surveyor intensified the field orientation exercises by taking the students further out into the forest. During these "safaris," two more pegmatites were found. The students were given one full day to examine the finds and submit individual plans of development. The best-prepared plans came from the two ex-soldiers. Each got to choose a crew of laborers to put his plan in practice. Soon, both pegmatites showed evidence of being economically mineralized.

The camp was beginning to look like the backyard of some museum due to the neat piles of various minerals placed in a wide swept area under large shade trees. The students spent long hours sitting around those piles with their notebooks in hand, memorizing the physical properties through which the minerals could be recognized. The most common valuable mineral was beryl. I had repeatedly told the students that it looked like quartz and could easily fool them.

One day the pickup returned from one of the newly discovered pegmatites, carrying some sacks that were immediately surrounded by the students. The sacks were full of large pieces of pink-colored beryl. I selected one chunk and said, "This is pink beryl, also called morganite. It is very easily mistaken for rose quartz, but rose quartz has little value whereas high quality morganite (deep-colored, completely transparent, and without flaws) can sell for one dollar per gram. That means one million dollars for a metric ton! So, make sure you learn to tell them apart. The luster of quartz is like that of ordinary glass; the luster of beryl is finer, more intense. Otherwise they both have practically the same specific gravity and hardness, and they both crystallize in the hexagonal system."

Zacarias came to me with a piece of morganite in his hand and said; "I saw an outcrop of this stuff before I came to work here. I thought it was rose quartz! If I show where it is, what will the company give me? I am serious!"

"I have no idea what the company will give you," I answered. "But the president will be visiting us soon, and you can talk to him. Do you have any samples to show him?"

"I did not bring any samples. But I know where I left them and can get them."

Three months after the "Malolo University" had opened its doors it was visited by the president of Monteminas. (In actual fact, the "University" did not have doors. To keep the inside temperature bearable, the classroom had a thatched grass roof and no walls.)

I called Zacarias, and he repeated what he had said to me. The president listened to the man and asked, "Is it outside our concession?"

"Yes, far from here. It is in the Gurué area. I went hunting with a friend last year. He drove all over the place looking for game. Then he stopped and asked me if the rocks in a nearby hill had any value. It was full of a mineral identical to the pink beryl we have here. I thought it was rose quartz and told the man so, but I took samples that were left in Gurué, and I can get them. If it is beryl, what will you offer for the find? I have to share it with the hunter."

"What I will do is this," said the president. "I will send up a Land Rover. When Mr. Bettencourt decides he can spare you, you can take the Land Rover and a driver and go find that hill again. Bring samples. If Mr. Bettencourt identifies them as beryl, we will register the find in the name of a new company in which you and your hunter friend can split a twenty-five percent share."

View of the Lice Valley from the front of my canvas tent, overlooking the campus of the "Malolo University." Photo by the author.

CHAPTER FOUR

One More Bridge to Build

In the Malolo pegmatite located near the camp, we had cut trenches that showed the pegmatite was zoned and well-mineralized. I proposed to the president of the company that we should move from development into mining, to start the students learning surface mining.

I already had a good idea of what each one of them would be able to accomplish. Of the twelve men, seven looked like they would be capable (with a lot of guidance) of managing a mine.

Malolo was on the left bank of the Lice River, while the other two finds of mineralized pegmatites were located on the opposite bank. All of the minerals that came from across the river were transported in sacks by porters who waded across, beating the water with sticks in order to keep the crocodiles respectful and at a safe distance.

I proposed building a bridge, and took the president to the site to explain how I intended to do it. He asked many questions, and we arrived at similar budget estimates. In the end he said, "I would not do it that way, but it makes sense and I am curious to see the result. Send me lists of what you need, and I will ship it to you immediately."

The following week, the students were divided into two groups. One, under the supervision of the surveyor, was put in charge of preparing field maps based on the aerial photographs the company had purchased. These photos covered most of the concession. Each map sheet represented a square of five by five kilometers and was plotted with all the information that could be seen in the photos. This would give the men as many points of reference in the field as possible.

I had already concluded a preliminary photo-geological interpretation of the area. Thus the surveyor was able to include on the maps recommendations to sample certain rock outcrops, in order to check my photo-interpretation. I esti-mated that this program would take about a month to complete, but it would give us a practical cartographic base to know where things were.

The other group was under my direction. They would be trained in surface mining methods, use of explosives, mine drainage, mine safety and hygiene, civil engineering principles, and how to work with tribesmen (who had to be taught almost everything with infinite patience).

I started them at the Malolo pegmatite. Firstly, I sent them into the bush to choose a location for the mine dump and then discussed with them the pros and cons of their choices. Next, came the drainage of the mine. I made them walk all over the surrounding bush to learn how the effluents from the mine would natu-rally flow when it rained.

When the drainage problems were understood, I made them choose a site for the workers' camp. Once they had determined where it should be built, I asked them to call the workers together, take them to the chosen site, and listen to their comments. There were some surprised faces when the Africans explained why they would not like to live at the site chosen. I said, "Remember that they under-stand the African environment far better than we do. So listen to their opinions carefully. It will save lots of headaches later."

So the lesson was driven home that in matters concerning the laborers' welfare, their customs and their beliefs, they should be consulted and included in the decisions. Otherwise you would probably make wrong decisions and have to do it all over again, like now. For Africa is Africa, and Africans have their own ways of coping with it.

The outcome was that the camp for the workers was built at the site that the workers chose.

With the help of Chief Novanana, with whom I visited regularly and for whom I developed respect and friendship, I recruited sixty new workers for the construction of the bridge. I ordered wheelbarrows, picks, shovels, crowbars, drilling steel, a hand-operated forge and blacksmith's tools, gasoline-driven water pumps, bags of cement, and reinforcing steel.

While awaiting the arrival of the materials, we built a warehouse to store them as well as a camp for the newly-arrived labor force. One of the students in my group had worked in construction, so I put him in charge of the preliminary operations, and later, during the construction phase, he became superintendent.

Up to this time, every one of the trainees had been responsible for the kitchen for one week at a time. He "planned" meals with the assistance of the cook, and kept an eye on purchases of supplies. Eventually, my turn as "kitchen supervisor" arrived. I met with the cook each evening to discuss the next day's meals, and completely forgot the subject after he went away.

A boy about fifteen, wearing his best clothes, had come to ask for work, and I had told him that he was too young to work in the mines. He just stood there with disappointment written all over his face and said he needed a job, that he could read and write, had studied at the mission, and it was too far to walk back home again. I felt sorry for him and said, "The only job I can give you is in the kitchen, helping the cook. You do not want that, do you?"

"Yes, sir, I do," said he.

"*Orrera pama* (it is well)," I replied. "Go to the kitchen, and tell Cuca that I sent you."

The next time I saw him, he was wearing a spotless white apron that was too long for him and a cylindrical white hat that was half as long as he was tall. He came to serve the evening meal in the dining room with a very serious manner, his bright, intelligent eyes checking every detail.

After my week as "kitchen supervisor" was over, the other "boarders" presented a petition to the effect that I should stay on permanently because the quality of the food had improved considerably during my stewardship. The truth of the matter was that I had not paid any attention to the kitchen and actually could not even remember the last time I had met with the cook. Now I decided, guiltily, to live up to my responsibilities, and went to tell him that his work was being appreciated and to encourage him to keep it up.

The only person I met in the kitchen was the young fellow, busily peeling potatoes.

"Hullo. What is your name?" I inquired.

He got up, made a bow to me, and answered, "I am Fernando João. I am Cuca, if you please."

"You mean you are helping the Cuca, don't you? Where is he?"

"No sir. The Cuca got very drunk after you sent me to work in the kitchen. He went home. He no come back. So, I cook. I learn in mission."

Not being able to think up any profound remarks *a propos* of the situation, I said, "Well, keep it up. But come to me in the evening for us to plan the meals, and when the cook returns, you send him to see me. I am truly curious to learn where he obtained the booze in a remote place like Malolo."

That evening, I told the others what had transpired. When Fernando came in to serve the soup wearing his usual oversized uniform, everybody complimented him. Somebody said, "Keep it up Muana Cuca," and the name stuck.[11] The cook never returned, and I sent the balance of his pay to Chief Novanana with a note explaining the facts. Muana Cuca continued to feed us, and well. He was given an assistant and a full cook's salary, and he was liked and respected by all.

After the crew recruited for the construction of the bridge had been installed in their camp, we cleared the bridge site of trees and bushes. The surveyor planted a series of markers in the ground to serve as reference points. I personally investigated the trees from which we intended to get the timber for the platform of the bridge and marked the suitable ones.

The next step was to dry up the river. This we did by first building a dividing dike made from loose rocks collected along the banks. The dike forced the water towards the far bank, leaving our side of the river almost dry. Then, the site of the abutment of the future bridge, nearest to the Malolo Camp, was surrounded by another dike. The water was pumped out, soil was excavated to bedrock, and the void was filled with concrete.

To build the first line of pillars that would support the deck of the bridge, we made a circular dike by piling sacks filled with clayey soil around the location. We kept the inside dry by sucking the water out constantly with the gasoline-driven water pumps. Then, we excavated down to bedrock inside the dammed space, built a platform of concrete which rested on bedrock, and set in place forty-four gallon drums with both lids removed. They were set vertically on the foundation. Then, reinforcing steel bars were placed in holes drilled into the bedrock and freshly mixed concrete was poured in until each drum was filled. Then, another drum was slid onto the top of the ones already in place and more reinforcing steel bars were tied to the original ones. A bamboo pole scaffold was built around the barrels which were filled by hand with concrete from buckets.

As soon as we had the first line of three pillars filled to the correct height, we installed three long, thick beams of hardwood on top of them. The tips of the steel bars protruding from the uppermost drums were bent around the beams, so as to fasten them solidly to the pillars.

The men learned their tasks quite rapidly, and the project went well. A little over three months after the concrete for the abutment on the left bank had been poured, we had completed the platform. It was made of wooden boards that we could drive the pickup truck over to carry heavy equipment needed for the abutment on the right bank.

The operation of weaving a bamboo mat was now started and continued at a slow but steady pace. Cars would roll over the mat, which would in turn prevent the wooden plank deck of the bridge from wearing out. Africans are great weavers, and the Achirima tribe was especially adept at making mats with bamboo.

When I drove across for the first time, the bamboo mat only covered about three-quarters of the platform. I stopped before reaching the end of the mat, to make sure I would not damage the work being done by the "weavers." They all stopped, started to clap their hands, and did an impromptu dance, which I joined. This was the "formal official opening ceremony" of the Lice Bridge.

(Since no one was running for political office, the press was dispensed with; television was still years in the future!)

I waited for the dancing and singing to end, thanked the performers, drove carefully to the opposite bank, and proceeded slowly along the ancient African road for a few miles until many windfalls across the road barred my way and made me turn around.

The next day I sent a group of men with axes and saws to clear the old trail. They were led by an experienced leader and took food for one week's stay.

In the meantime, I was busy getting the Malolo mine into production and supervising the development of two other mineral deposits found by the men, while the surveyor was teaching them the art of orientation in the jungle. I decided it was time to send Zacarias on the promised trip to locate the "hill of pink beryl" that he was convinced he had found in the Gurué area. He took a Land Rover with a full tank of gas, plus another eighty liters of fuel in boxes[12] for the return trip.

Towards the end of the week, I went to investigate how far the workers had progressed with the task of clearing the African road. There had been some distant thunder during the two previous nights and it had rained for a couple of hours, but the weather was clear when I crossed the bridge and drove towards the southeast. The road presented a hard, smooth surface. It followed the high ground between the valleys of the Lice and Melela Rivers, and I could see in the distance prominent mountains sticking out above the forest cover.

The car assistant pointed out Mount Uapé and Mount Morrua, towards which the road was headed. Both were prominent inselbergs[13] that constituted excellent navigational markers. On both sides of the road were tall trees of many species, growing a good distance from each other and permitting the existence of many flowering bushes, palms, and grasses. Creepers adhering to the trunks of the tallest trees gave the forest a look of tropical exuberance, and wild orchids clung to the shady sides of the tree trunks. However, when I stopped and walked a short distance into the forest, I realized that the tropical look was an illusion. The patches of luxuriant vegetation were small and spaced far apart. The forest was in reality a typical "park forest," in which many different species grow, spaced tens of meters apart from each other, allowing plenty of sunlight to penetrate to the surface of the ground.

After traveling nearly twenty-five kilometers, I met our party at work with machetes and axes, swinging their tools to the rhythm of improvised songs directed by their leader. I asked how far it was to Morrua.

"There was a hunting party that came by yesterday," replied the *capataz*.[14] "They had been sent out from Chief Napido's tribe. They explained to us that just before you get to Napido's village, at a place called Nantala, this road branches to the north. It goes by the Uapé Mountain, and then on to Gilé which is on the right bank of the Molócuè River. Right now, we are about halfway to Nantala. Another branch of the road goes past the abandoned Old Morrua Fort, then crosses the Melela River and continues on to the southwest for a very long distance until it reaches Mulevala. But people do not travel that way, unless they are in large groups. The old fort is haunted."

I took the men back with me. They were all excited, turning their heads from one side of the car to the other; they had never been in a motorcar. When we got near the bridge one of them explained something to the car assistant, who translated that the man had "heard the river roaring." Less than one kilometer further, I turned right onto the approach road to the bridge and saw that the water was almost up to the top of the structure.

The new bridge over the Lice River faces its first challenge. The river is at flood stage, and one of the prospectors is trying to clear away branches that have been carried downstream. Photo by the author.

Moments later, water covered the bridge and several of us were stranded on the "wrong" side with the car. The waters receded after several hours, and we were finally able to walk across. Photo by the author.

I stopped, and we joined one of the prospectors who was on the bridge trying to clear away tree branches. They had been carried down by the flood and were jammed on the upstream side. I sent one of the men to camp to bring as many workers as possible with saws and axes so we could attempt to clear the pavement of debris that might damage it.

By the time the men arrived, the water was over the pavement. The car and the men who had traveled with me were isolated on the wrong side of the Lice. They just sat down watching the floodwaters go by until, hours later, the bridge emerged from the waters enough for them to cross and come to the Malolo Camp. I did not dare drive the car across until the next day, after the bridge had been carefully inspected and some repairs carried out on the woven bamboo mat. The flood had been caused by the thunderstorms we had heard the day before, raging far away.

CHAPTER FIVE

Armed Invasion

As soon as access to the central part of the concession was possible over the Lice Bridge, systematic prospecting finally got under way. Each man was given an area of five by five kilometers that he had to criss-cross in every direction, observing its geological composition, taking samples, making notes and checking for signs of mineralization. The prospectors were each equipped with a canvas tent, a bed, a table, one chair, cooking utensils, tools of various kinds, and lots of sample bags. Each was accompanied by eight tribesmen, recruited from the nearby villages, and a messenger with a bicycle. The prospectors would stay in contact with my headquarters via their messengers.

All the geological information reported on weekly reports had to be backed by samples that were correctly numbered, referenced in each prospector's notebook, and plotted on his map. Samples were packed in baskets woven from local reeds, which the messengers carried on their bicycles. All samples ended up on the shelves of the lab in areas reserved for each prospector. Every day I checked the prospector's reports and wrote notes verifying or correcting the field classifications. When I came across samples that might be of interest, I set a date to visit the occurrence in the company of the prospector responsible for the find. A messenger, on his bicycle, took a note from me announcing the visit.

When Zacarias returned from his trip to find the lost morganite mine, one look at his face told me he had not been successful. "What happened?" I asked.

"Everything went wrong," said he. "The hunter I had gone with has died. The widow said she wrote to me, but I did not receive her letter. So, I and the driver drove all over that bush but I never saw that hill again!"

"Well," I replied, "you tried your best. It probably was rose quartz, anyway. You may have better luck the next time. I am sorry your partner died."

"I am sorry about his death also," answered Zacarias. "But as for the rose quartz, I recovered the samples I had put away." He opened his field pack and handed me two nice pieces of morganite beryl, each the size of a fist.

I examined them carefully and said, "You really had bad luck: this is very good morganite!"

"I knew you would say that! I hope I will have better luck finding mines for this company than I did for myself!"

I put him in charge of the Malolo Mine. The mine's production of beryl and tantalite increased steadily from month to month. We had a sizable pile of beryl neatly arranged in the shape of a square pyramid. Near to it was a sturdy platform made of bamboo, where fifty-kilogram bags of tantalite were piled neatly. The Malolo Pegmatite produced a tetragonal dimorph of tantalite called tapiolite, very rich in tantalum, that was worth nearly $20,000 per ton. There was a small fortune on top of that shelf!

The Malolo pegmatite. The first trenches that were cut showed that it was zoned. Beryl pieces are exposed at the bottom of the central trench where the men are working. Photo by the author.

After the students graduated and were assigned individual jobs away from Malolo, the campus underwent some changes. The classroom became the laboratory. It had shelves covered with mineral and rock samples on three sides, and the fourth was occupied by instruments and chemicals used in assaying minerals. Nearby was the re-modeled kitchen (smaller now, but better equipped). Behind the kitchen, at the edge of the camp, was an ample chicken coop. It was kept open during the day to let the chickens forage for food, but locked tightly during the night to frustrate leopards and foxes.

The surveyor, Zacarias, and two other men who were learning mining methods at Malolo, had their tents on the entrance side of the camp, near a hut built especially to house visitors. We all ate together. My tent was located at the extreme end of the camp, overlooking the Lice valley, under the shade of tall trees where it was quiet and there was a cool breeze. Nearby was the radio shack. Between this installation and my tent was a grass-roofed cage made of bamboo and raised two feet above the ground. There, I kept two baby leopards.

One of the prospectors, who had been a professional hunter before he joined us, was visited in his camp one night by a leopard. His African assistants were frightened and pressured him to backtrack the animal, in order to find out where it came from and why it had entered their camp. They followed the spoor to some rocks where they saw the leopard, and were distracted because it made a stand, and displayed signs of intention to defend its territory and readiness to attack them.

The prospector was forced to shoot the animal, and, while examining it afterwards noticed that it was a female with the teats full of milk. This made them search amongst the rocks to be sure that the male was not hiding and ready to attack their camp during the night. They found the den she had been trying to defend. It was home to two cubs about the size of domestic cats. There were no signs of a male adult (usually the female leopard rears the cubs alone and moves them to new dens every couple of days), but, when dealing with leopards, experienced men like this one who had been a professional hunter, do not take anything at face value. He used cloth sample bags to cover the cubs and to protect himself from their sharp claws, and carried them to his camp. His intentions were to find out whether the male was in the vicinity, or not. If he were nearby, he would attempt to steal the cubs and carry them away during the next night.

Everybody was alert that night, but nothing happened. The workers' nerves calmed down and everything returned to normal. But the prospector had no facilities to raise the cubs, and he knew that other predators would kill them if he returned them to the den. The only person who might take care of them and who had a permanent camp, was me. So, he covered the cubs with a gunnysack, put them in a woven basket which he tied to the back of his bicycle, and came to my camp.

I was not overjoyed with the gift, or with the idea of having to bottle-feed two snarling, clawing and biting little wild devils, equipped with sharp claws and teeth. But I was not going to let them die, either. So, I paid some men to build a safe bamboo cage for the cubs. I sent one of the drivers to ask the matron of the maternity at Novanana for the loan of a baby feeding bottle and advice on what milk formula I should prepare.

The author handling two orphaned leopard cubs at the Malolo Camp. The essential equipment when caring for them included muleskin gloves and infinite patience. Photo by the author.

I had plenty of powdered milk and a pair of thick muleskin gloves to protect my hands from their sharp claws. The only other assets needed for a successful attempt at being mother to the two growling little devils, were a lot of patience and luck.

I fed the cubs, one at a time, every morning and evening and had to keep all my attention on the job to avoid being painfully bitten or clawed. In the evening I got them out of their cage, put leashes on them, and walked them around the camp for exercise. Invariably, they pulled away towards the forest as hard as they could and tried to get into bushes to hide. Another interesting reaction was that of the chickens that moved around freely in the camp during the day. On seeing the cubs, they would raise their feathers, let out cackles of alarm, and run away as fast as their legs and raised wings could take them. This happened, even though the leopards paid not the slightest attention to them.

Many local peasants came to the camp to offer vegetables and fruits for sale. They sometimes came accompanied by their dogs, which, if they happened to see the cubs or even to smell them, immediately let out yelps of alarm and ran back up the trail with their tails between their legs. You were left with no doubts about who had hunted whom, for thousands of years past, leopards having a strong appetite for chicken and for dog meat.

As soon as the cubs were given to me, I wrote to the American Consul in Lourenço Marques and asked if he could indicate a zoo in the U.S. that might be interested in obtaining, free of charge, the two cubs. Local zoos were pretty well stocked and were not interested. He answered some weeks later that a zoo in Ohio was interested, and arrangements were being made for the cubs to be collected.

Unfortunately, when the news reached me, it was too late! The rainy season had started; nights were hot and muggy, bringing with them the ideal conditions for armies of carrier ants to start marching. Carrier ants, also known as army ants and as *talaakwa* in the Achirima language, usually move to new nests at night when the weather is hot and the humidity is high. They appear as long, dark red ribbons of insects marching shoulder-to-shoulder, varying in width up to two feet and over one mile in length. The center of the formation is made up of small ants that carry on their backs eggs, larvae, seeds and other supplies, and an uninterrupted line of soldiers guards the flanks. These specialized security guards are over one inch long and come armed with formidable pincers capable of cutting grass stems and killing other insects, and of inflicting very painful bites on humans.

Our camp was in a large area cleared of all grass and bushes, in order to discourage ants, snakes, field mice, tarantulas and centipedes from approaching the tents. Up until now we had not suffered from any inconveniences caused by the insect population. Because I lived at the very end of the camp close to the forest,

I always kept a flashlight, plus my boots and the loaded rifle, inside the mosquito net that enclosed my cot. The net served the purpose of stopping flying insects, and the diversified collection of spiders of all sizes that followed them, from getting inside.

Although dangerous animals could easily get into a canvas tent by tearing the cloth open, they didn't. There were ropes stretched all around to keep each tent up. Due to the humidity of the atmosphere during the tropical nights, these ropes became so taut that they made a twang-like sound if touched. Apparently, this was why animals kept away from tents. It is generally accepted that the ropes awaken in their memories countless traps set by man to catch wild animals for thousands of years past. Many a time I have heard the "twang" of a rope touched by some animal moving in the dark, immediately followed by the thud produced as the animal jumped away and landed further out.

I have always been a sound sleeper when all the sounds of the night are normal. The African forest is never quiet at night. There are birds that hunt and call to each other; there are insects humming away all the time; monkeys, as well as the ever present baboons, keep up a constant racket; lemurs screech all night; and all kinds of other small animals add their noisy signatures to the background noise.

All these sounds are normal, and my subconscious became used to them long ago. But let a lion roar, a leopard cough, or a hyena let out its irritating laugh, and I would be instantly wide-awake, my senses on the alert and listening to identify the origin of the danger—the sound that had woke me.

That night I woke up with the rifle in my hand (something that had only happened a few times before in my life). I listened for a while to try and identify what was out there. But there were no sounds from nearby. Besides the baboons, barking far away, there were no sounds at all: I could hear no birds, not even insects chirping. It was dead quiet, and ominously frightening!

Something out there was terrifying all animals. They were all quiet, but on the alert for some danger: something really bad that monopolized their attention. And I better be ready for it, whatever it might be. So I fumbled for my boots, found them in the dark, pulled the tail of the mosquito netting from under the mattress, swung my feet out and into the boots, got the flashlight from under the pillow with my left hand and the rifle out from under the mosquito net with my right hand, slid the safety catch of the rifle to the firing position and turned the flash light on, inspecting the corners of the tent first. There was nothing there. But I felt there was something. Something was different.

It was frightening, and I felt an urgent compulsion to find out what it was, to identify the unseen *enemy*. As I moved the beam of the flashlight around the inside of the tent once again, I saw it: the mosquito net, which was white, had turned to a dark red color and had become opaque. It was covered with *talaakwa*, the dreaded army ants. They were concentrated on the mosquito netting, aware of my smell, and were trying to get at me. Others were covering my clothes (which still hung on the chair). I put the rifle and the electric torch against the cot where I had been sleeping and, without thinking, started the routine of putting my clothes on before I opened the front flap of the tent, as I did every morning. The *talaakwa* started to bite me as soon as they crawled over the outside of my clothes! I felt the intense pain of their bites and started to beat at them with both hands. While my hands worked in a frenzy that attracted more ants and made them more excited, my brain was starting to take command of the situation—to rationalize, to analyze the unexpected situation, and to look for a solution. I realized that I had to awaken the other men in camp. There was no point in yelling, for they were too far away to hear me. It became clear that I had to go near their tents to call them out.

As I undid the lacing ropes of the tent in order to open up the front flap, I picked up a number of ants that immediately sank their scissor-like mandibles into my arms. I ran out as soon as I had unlaced the front of the tent, and raced towards the other tents. I woke up the surveyor and grabbed a hammer to beat on the steel bar we had hung from a tree. This bar was used in the mornings to rouse the African workers in their camp, which lay some distance away.

The pain on my legs and arms was excruciating. Many dozens of ants were embedded in my hide. But there was nothing I could do right away that could ease the pain.

As the men came out of their tents I explained what was happening and told them to get their kerosene lanterns lighted. I ordered them to organize themselves and the African workers into groups and get buckets from the warehouse, which they would fill with diesel fuel. Next, they were to make brooms out of tree branches and start sprinkling diesel over the areas covered by the ants. I told them to hang the lanterns from tree branches to give us some light, but to hang them high enough to avoid causing fires.

I got a bucket, filled it with diesel fuel and started to rub the liquid over my arms while telling the others to do the same. By the light of the lanterns we could see that the ants had spread out over about half of the camp, including the kitchen, the dining room, and all the way to my tent. The other half, where the men's tents, the warehouses, the garages, and the "filling station" were located, had not been overrun.

Somebody had the idea of forming a bucket brigade that slowly advanced over a wide front, sprinkling diesel fuel over the ants—and on ourselves when we started to feel the painful bites. Empty buckets came back again and again, to be replenished. In some places, the concentration of ants was such that the ground was completely covered. If there was no danger of it getting out of hand, fire was applied to the fuel over these patches. The fires were under the supervision of one of the African leaders, who put them out as soon as the ants had been roasted.

The battle went on without rest until dawn broke, and by the increasing light I made an inspection of the whole area. It was then that I remembered the leopard cubs and ran to their cage, which was located near my tent. They were huddled together in one corner and seemed dead. There were ants all over the inside of the cage. When I opened the gate and picked up one cub by the scruff of the neck, it uttered a weak sound like the meow of a cat, but did not move. When I looked more closely, I saw that in place of its little round belly there was a gaping hole filled with ants. They had eaten away the innards of the poor little creature! The other cub was in the same condition.

With tears running down my face, I ran to my tent. I opened the steel trunk and took out a target-shooting pistol, loaded it, and returned to the cage. I shot each of the cubs in the head to end its suffering.

Inside the chicken coop, there were heaps of feathers and bones stripped clean of meat and skin. Inside the small storeroom where we had kept our food supplies we found gunnysacks neatly cut open and completely empty, where our potatoes, dried peas, rice, and beans had been stored. Only a sack of coarse salt was intact. The clean bone of a smoked ham hung from the roof on a hand-woven string.

Naturally, the ants had not managed to get inside the many tins of canned food. But every can that had had a paper label glued to it was clean. The ants had eaten the labels, leaving us unable to distinguish whether a can contained dried milk, canned peaches or corned beef!

The ants that make up these armies are all females of various shapes and sizes. They are effectively "mass-produced" in accordance with a genetic code that supplies insects which are especially built to perform the functions needed to maintain the welfare of the colony. Scouts move in front of the columns, choosing the paths to follow and the victims to attack. Next come the engineers that smooth the path for the main body of the army. They remove small rocks and cut grass down to the level of the ground and remove it from the path. Behind the army, for hours after it has passed by a place, one can see the stragglers—the old, the sick, and the wounded—stubbornly following.[15]

After the invasion was defeated, we were left with a camp that stank of burnt ants and diesel fuel. Patches of ground were blackened by ashes where we had set fire to thicker concentrations of *talaakwa*.

CHAPTER SIX

International Trade

Most of the prospecting work was now taking place to the east, and the three mines that we had in operation near the camp were run quite well by former students of the "Malolo University" who could take care of themselves. They had already reached the stage of having their own staff, their own workshops, and camps for their workers. I visited the mines regularly and was quite satisfied with the way they were being operated.

The invasion of *talaakwa* accelerated the decision to move to a more centrally located site. I talked with the president over the radio, told him of the invasion, and suggested that instead of wasting a lot of time cleaning and repairing Malolo, I would prefer to establish a permanent camp somewhere near Chief Napido's village, in an area I had already visited. It had good road access, there was a permanent spring nearby, and it was near an African road that ran northward. This road promised to become a good means of accessing the center of the concession. He agreed and promised to send two pre-fabricated houses, one for the office and laboratory and the other for me to live in.

In the first days of 1959, I visited Novanana to say good-bye to the old chief who had been a good neighbor, and on whose counsel I had relied for the solution of so many problems.

We moved during the next weekend. All my requirements were packed in the big truck, which followed closely behind me in the Beetle. There was enough room in the truck for Muana Cuca, his kitchen assistants, and the lab assistant. All the other African personnel who had been recruited from Chief Novanana's subjects were sent to the operating mines or stayed with the surveyor. There was no need to carry our large stock of chickens. They had been eaten by the *talaakwa*!

After checking with Chief Napido on arrival, I explained that we intended to set up a permanent headquarters, and he indicated that the *cabo de terras*[16] would come with me. This functionary suggested that the best location to establish a base camp was a plateau that had some tall shade trees, was close to a natural spring, and had not been awarded to any African family. We walked all over it, checked the direction of the predominant winds, and inspected the vegetation and the soil composition. I asked him questions about whether there were mosquitoes, tsetse flies, killer bees, termites, snakes, or poisonous plants such as crazy beans.[17] All the answers were negative: the area seemed as good for installing a permanent camp as you would be likely to find.

Just to make sure that he was not, for reasons of his own, trying to "sell me" this location, I asked, "How about lions, leopards, hyenas and wild dogs?"

He looked me straight in the eyes, and answered, "All your other questions were important things to know about this location, and they show me that you know Africa. So, you must also know that, since we have goats, we have lions and leopards. If you have lions and leopards, you will have hyenas living off the scraps that those leave behind. One does not have to point this out. That is the way Africa is. As for wild dogs, no, we do not have them here."

This exchange showed me that the *cabo de terras* was no fool and that he did not intend to take any foolishness from me either. So, I accepted his suggestion for locating our camp there, thanked him, and drove him in the Beetle back to his village.

Before the end of the week, we had installed all the facilities necessary, cleaned up the area around a permanent spring that was to become our water supply, and cut a short road from the camp to intersect with the Malolo trail. We had also cleared and leveled the sites for the two pre-fabricated houses and had chosen the locations for garages, maintenance shops, warehouses, the first aid station (which in time grew to become a five bed hospital), the minerals treatment plant, housing for employees, the power plant, a school for employees' children, the sports ground and a rubbish dump.

We already had three mines in regular production and another three that were being developed. Even during the development stage they produced valuable minerals, which were stored in individual piles in the Malolo warehouses.

Export of minerals from Mozambique had long been done in a haphazard fashion. A few mineral brokers visited the mines once a year and made offers in cash for the existing stocks. No long-term contracts existed, nor did the producers always respect the specifications set by the buyers. As a result, the prices paid by buyers were generally low.

Foreseeing that the management would want to sell the stocks we had accumulated, I had sent representative samples for formal assaying to U.S. laboratories.

The results indicated that we could export beryl ore containing above twelve percent beryllium oxide. This was a good bargaining point because exports from Mozambique had previously always run about ten percent. Our columbite also assayed above the average, while the tantalite coming out of the Malolo mine was a rare variety—called Tapiolite—and was very rich in tantalum.

When the president said over the radio that he thought we should start to sell some of the minerals in storage, I answered that I would send him a proposal for a plan to be followed in future.

The plan was to offer American buyers regular shipments at agreed specifications and prices. If we shipped minerals assaying above the agreed specs, we wanted to receive bonuses. For failure to meet the contractual specs we were prepared to pay penalties at twice the amount set for the bonuses. But we wanted to have the right to cancel any contract as soon as we wished, after three satisfactory shipments had been made.

Our first offer to an American buyer was twenty tons per month of plus ten percent beryl, for $250 per metric ton (F.O.B. Pebane harbor). Pebane was the closest port to our mines that was visited regularly by American freighters. The offers for columbite and tantalite were also for very high-grade ores.

These prices were higher than other Mozambican exporters were getting, and the prospective buyer wrote back informing us that they were prepared to accept the offer but at lower prices, because their experience showed that Mozambican exporters seldom met the agreed specifications. They were prepared to accept the bonuses and penalty clauses. I suggested to the president of our firm that we should accept this offer, because I had in stock more than enough to meet three shipments and the production of the mines was steadily improving.

In every shipment made under the terms of this contract, we surpassed the agreed assays and received bonuses. After the third shipment of each kind of mineral, we informed the buyers that we were canceling the contracts, as we considered the prices to be too low. We would only be prepared to sign new contracts if they were for larger monthly shipments and at ten percent higher prices.

We were offered a five percent increase in prices, which we accepted. But we again cancelled the contracts after the third shipment, saying the prices were too low. We indicated that we were prepared to increase the monthly shipments, but only if the prices were increased by ten percent. This time we received a long letter in response, pointing out that if they paid us what we were asking, they would have to pay higher prices to the other suppliers as well.

The president's answering letter was a little masterpiece. He thanked them for showing appreciation for our efforts to produce better quality ores in larger amounts. He said he was sorry to see they had not understood a key point: our good results came from increased investment on our part, which translated into higher production costs. He ended by saying that since we could not reduce our costs by producing minerals of inferior quality, he saw no other solution than for the buyers to pay for the improvement in quality. As for the probability that other exporters would also ask for more money, he did not think that was a significant risk for them to take. Had it not occurred to them that it could turn out a lot worse if we started to buy the production of the others and then forced the buyers to pay our increased prices?!

From then on, instead of canceling contracts after three shipments, we resorted to reminding the buyers regularly of what they were paying to Brazilian producers. We obtained offers that were close seconds, because we were approaching the position of second-largest beryl producer in Africa. The buyers had now learned that we knew the prices they were paying for Brazilian ores, and they had developed a healthy respect for our president's ability to call their hands and to bargain with them.

CHAPTER SEVEN

The Swamp

It began to take more and more time to keep the prospecting operation running smoothly, while simultaneously increasing production from the operating mines. I was running short of hours during my work days, and I had to hand the daily chores of the mining operation over to the surveyor. I retained responsibility for planning of all operations, evaluation of the reports submitted by the prospectors, and relations with the local authorities.

I read every report sent in by every prospector, and studied the mineral specimens and rocks that accompanied them. Then I would pull out the master sheet for the respective area, color in the geology, and write down the names of the streams or hills mentioned in the prospector's report. Sometimes there were descriptions of the local geology that merited further investigation; other reports confirmed geological conclusions that I had already made. Finally, I would sit at the stereoscope table and study how specific rock formations, identified in the field, looked on the aerial photographs. I was always searching for any anomalous sign that might give me a clue to mineralized areas.

As promised, we received two disassembled pre-fabricated houses. I immediately put one up to house the office and laboratory. Our laboratory had all the necessaries for performing most tests to identify minerals. I could even do a gold assay by the amalgamation method. But the most common tests we performed were specific gravity tests to identify beryl, because the specific gravity of beryl is only slightly higher than that of quartz (which it resembles very closely). To economize on time and be certain that the lab work was conducted thoroughly and competently, I had sent for Pampuela. He was the young prospector I had trained while I was in charge of the operations at the Alto Ligonha Mines,[18] and I had

41

coached him on how to perform the usual tests needed to identify minerals. He had learned to do these quite well.

Next, we assembled my house. An office and radio shack occupied most of the space, leaving just enough room for a small bedroom and tiny dining room. At the back, in another small building made of hand-shaped, sun-dried adobe bricks, were a bathroom and a small compartment for the electric generator.

The kitchen occupied an individual small building, in order to limit the progress of any fires that might start there. Some distance away, there was a classic "leopard-proof chicken coop." Or so I believed, until I was rudely proven wrong one morning when Fernando informed me with a very sad face that during the night *havarra*[19] had managed to get inside the chicken coop, kill all the chickens, and eat dozens of them.

"I am sorry," he said, "but you will now have only the first half of bacon and eggs: that is, bacon without eggs!"

Fernando's command of the Portuguese language was excellent, and he loved to use it with a dry sense of humor. Like most Achirima, he considered the local subjects of Chief Napido (who were of mixed Lomwe-Achirima extraction) to be somewhat inferior, and he had turned up his nose at the way they had built the chicken coop. He had, in fact, offended the builders by commenting that it would only protect the chickens if the leopards in this area were like the local inhabitants: a little stupid!

After his comments I had inspected the building carefully, and I also noticed details which showed a lack of respect for the uncanny ability of leopards to break into shelters built to protect live animals. But, to avoid an outbreak of tribal rivalry, I had not criticized the construction errors. Now I was paying for my negligence and for not calling the builders to task, by having to go without eggs for breakfast. Plus, I had to put up with Fernando's veiled sarcasm and the added burden of having to shoot a thieving leopard before it got into the habit of attacking my egg supply every time he felt like having a meal at my expense!

The rest of the camp was also progressing. We had started to build a large shed for vehicle and machinery maintenance and another for the minerals treatment plant, when I received a visit from two old friends. One was the son of a gold prospector I had known back in the early forties. At that time, he had been just a teenager who spent all his time keeping his dad's old pick-up truck in running condition.

He told me that his father had since passed away, but he still owned and drove the antique truck (it was so old it had wooden spokes in the wheels). He explained that he had learned to be a motorcar mechanic through the need to keep it running. He had never been to school and did not have any certificates, but could fix and maintain all makes of cars and mining machinery. He wondered if I would give him a job and, in fact, I was happy to do so. His name was Nunes, and he was known as Nunes Surdo. *Surdo* means deaf—though I had never noticed his deafness, he was so good at reading my lips.

The other visitor had also been an employee of the Alto Ligonha Mines at the time I was their director. His name was also Nunes, and he known as Nunes Sondador (*sondador* means driller). He also wanted a job. I had planned to carry out a program of routine checks for alluvial gold, by drilling in the banks of the main streams to check for the presence of that metal. I gave him a job as a prospector until we got a drilling machine.

The two men arrived just in time to inherit my canvas tent, as I moved into my new "residence." The tent stayed in the same place where I had erected it, but they added a wooden plaque in which they carved "2 Nunes Palace."

Among the maps of areas under scrutiny, there was a geological sheet that included a swampy area. In the middle of the swamp was an isolated hill. As I pulled out geological sheets to add information sent in by the prospectors, an unusual occurrence of a fairly large, isolated hill in the middle of a swamp aroused my curiosity. It was unusual, and unusual occurrences are the kind of phenomena that catch the attention of geologists. In the aerial photographs, I could see that the swamp was extensive and the hill looked like the outcrop of a large pegmatite. The area was far from any roads, which meant it had to be approached on foot; I did not have the time to do that.

I showed the map to Nunes Sondador and carefully coached him on our prospecting system. I gave him thirty men and all the necessary paraphernalia, and instructed him to "Cut a road to the edge of the swamp, try to cross the water to the hill, take a good look for mineralization, and send me a report." Then he took off with the shared canvas tent, leaving Nunes Surdo to double up with the office clerk.

His first reports indicated that he had managed to find the correct location of the swamp and was inspecting the area to find the best course for a road to reach it. He also reported seeing various outcrops of pegmatites, all of them mineralized with beryl and columbite. In this area the prospectors were not expected to be able to distinguish between tantalite and columbite, because the minerals occurred as a series of compounds. At one end there was tantalite, which contained close to the maximum possible tantalum allowed by the mineral's chemical formula, plus a little columbium. The composition varied with increasing concentrations of columbium (and less and less tantalum), until the minerals were identified as columbite. So, the prospectors referred to any very dense, black mineral as columbite. It was up to me, when I got their samples, to run tests in the lab and identify them as tantalum, columbium, or tin minerals. The presence of any one of these made me more and more curious, because all were extremely valuable.

Finally, Nunes Sondador's messenger arrived one day, carrying a large basket of samples on the back of his bicycle. He also carried a report from Nunes announcing that the road I had asked to be cut had reached the swamp. Nunes reported that he had found a ford in the middle of the swamp, which made it possible to access the hill. He had already waded across and walked all over the hill, and had verified that it was a pegmatite. He had observed that it was zoned and it had a long and wide quartz core. Unfortunately, he had seen no beryl. The shallow pits he had dug at various points showed no heavy minerals, but he thought I had better come and see it in person.

The report showed that he had carefully observed all the clues that he had found, even noticing that the pegmatite was zoned. Although I was somewhat disappointed that he had not seen any mineralization, I had a persisting feeling that there was something which had not been completely studied. I had to see for myself. I sent the messenger back the next day with a note saying that I would visit two days hence.

I took the surveyor with me, so he could plot the new road on the maps. After a cup of coffee with Nunes at his camp, we drove to the end of the trail and left the Land Rover in a clearing at the edge of the swamp.

In front of us was an expanse of dark water, across which Nunes had hammered down bamboo poles to mark the sinuous course of a ford. He took the lead, beating on the water all the time with a stick to keep crocodiles respectfully away. The water came up to our waists in some places, and it took about half an hour to get to the hill that was covered with sparse forest and presented a rocky surface. We put our boots and clothes back on, and I started to re-check the places where Nunes had taken his samples and the shallow pits he had dug.

Finding no traces of mineralization in any of the places I checked, I climbed to the top of the hill and observed that the crest of it was an extensive zone of quartz that had produced abundant, angular pieces of all sizes, strewn down the flanks. But, as had happened elsewhere, there was not a trace of any other mineralization besides the ever-present quartz and the occasional pieces of feldspars that are so common in pegmatites.

I was looking at one of the places where Nunes had chiseled out a sample, when the surveyor grabbed my shoulder and pointed in the direction where we had crossed to the hill. I looked and saw a grass fire moving quickly towards the point where I had parked the car. I started running down the slope of the hill and heard the others following me. It felt like it was a long downhill race to reach the swamp, and it seemed like it took hours more to cross the dark and muddy water. Towards the other side I found myself inside a cloud of smoke, tears running down my face. I was coughing and choking, but I finally made it to dry land where the fire had already passed, leaving clumps of grass and some green bushes smoking. This was the place where I had parked the Land Rover, but the car was not there!

My first thought was that I was in the wrong place. But I could see where the road ended and I also saw the imprints of the tires where the car had been. So I turned back down the track, running as fast as I could in my water-soaked boots. A few hundred yards further, I rounded a curve and saw that the fire had cut across the road leaving behind unburned bushes. And further along, there was the car! Standing by the Land Rover, with a very worried look on his face, was the car assistant.

"I am sorry," he said. "I do not learn how to change gears. When I see fire is coming towards where we were, I get inside; I pressed that pedal like you always do before you start the engine of the car. I manage to start the engine of the car. But when I take my foot off that pedal, the car started to run backwards and I no know how to turn it around. So I drive backwards up to here. But I bang against a tree and I break the back light. I pay out of my salary, please!"

I grabbed his hand and said, "You do not pay anything out of your salary. You get a month's salary as a bonus! You saved this car. And I am very grateful for what you did!"

The others arrived then, their clothes soaked and muddy. Like me, they had not stopped to change before they hit the swamp. That was when I realized that I was in the same state as they were. We took our clothes off, then, wrung the water out of them, and spread them over the bushes to dry in the sun. It was getting late, though, and we had to put them back on before they dried.

We drove back in wet clothes and reached Napido quite late. I went into the bathroom, took off my clothes, took a shower, put on a pair of pajamas, had a cup of coffee that Muana Cuca had brewed for me, ate a slice of bread with butter and fell into bed.

I spent most of the following morning with the crew that was building the minerals treatment plant. After lunch, I examined the specimens that had accumulated on the shelves of the lab. When I got to a small pile made up of three pieces of quartz, without a number tag, I started to give the lab assistant a tongue-lashing.

"I trained you to do this job very carefully, so that everything would be done correctly and so that there would be no confusion. You know that every specimen which comes into the lab has to have identification, and that you have to immediately contact—"

"But sir—" he interrupted.

"There are no 'buts,'" I continued. "You know the rules!"

I was about to continue on the same tack when he said, "You brought these samples in yourself. They were in the pocket of your pants. Muana Cuca found them in your wet clothes and brought them here this morning. So I keep for you to look at. I wait for you to tell what number I put on them. When you tell me, I put number tag on them."

Then I remembered that when the fire scare made me run for the car, I had been examining pieces of rock that had been chiseled by Nunes out of the core of the pegmatite. I had automatically put them in my pocket as I started to run.

I took a good look at them with the magnifying glass. "Very strange-looking quartz," I said to Pampuela. "And, before I forget, I am sorry I yelled at you!"

"Break one of these pieces into small fragments in the mortar. Then do a specific gravity test on one of those fragments, while I check to see whether the other pieces float or sink in bromoform."

Both tests showed that the mineral had a specific gravity higher than that of quartz. And, at that point, I became excited. I could not control my eagerness.

"Let's do a test," I said. "You grind one of the pieces into a fine powder while I set up the pressure stove and the muffle."

The test took us the rest of the afternoon. The other personnel working at their various jobs in camp closed up for the day. They came by and, sensing our excitement, asked what was going on. I told them I was suspicious that the "quartz" found at the pegmatite in the swamp might be beryl. And if it really was beryl, there was a fortune in that hill.

I asked them to get their kerosene pressure lamps lighted and bring them to the lab. It would be getting dark soon, and I did not want to interrupt the test. There was a small electric generator that was used to power the radio transmitter, but it was not connected to the laboratory. And the diesel generator that eventually lit the houses and streets of Napido would not be installed until later—with funds that came from the production of the Namivo Mine. This was the name given to the mineral deposit encountered in the middle of the swamp; but, I am getting ahead of my story.

We forgot dinner. After a while, Muana Cuca arrived carrying a tray loaded with sandwiches and a Thermos flask filled with hot coffee, which were shared with everybody.

The quinalizarine test consists of fusing a sample of the powdered mineral, putting the fused mass into solution, and then adding a drop of a solution of a purple-colored organic reagent called quinalizarine. In the presence of beryl, the reagent changes to a blue color.

When all the preparations had been made, we filtered the solution and divided it into three glass test tubes. I examined one, Pampuela looked at another and

Nunes Surdo looked at the third one. Almost at the same time we each exclaimed, "It is blue!"

When I went back to the swamp the next day, Nunes Sondador was not in his camp. He had left early to do his prospecting and, therefore, could not go with us to the "hill in the middle of the swamp." The surveyor, Pampuela, and I collected a few kilos of representative samples, taken along the length of the "quartz ridge" that outcropped along the top of the hill. I left a note for Nunes, explaining what was up and instructing him to cut a prospecting trench at right angles to the trend of the ridge, and from one side of the hill to the other.

Back in the lab, I prepared a composite sample to be sent to a reputable laboratory in South Africa. On the next radio call to the president I told him, "We have urgent need of the medicines I requested from you yesterday. Could you please send them by plane to Alto Molócuè airfield tomorrow? I will be waiting from ten in the morning to receive them."

He asked me to repeat the message, and I did.

Then he said, "My secretary is a good practical nurse. Do you want him to come and advise on the treatment?"

I answered, "I think it would be a good idea. I will meet him personally at Alto Molócuè."

In our code, this meant that I had an important message for him and wanted to send it by a responsible person. He knew I had not requested any medicines. The mention that his secretary was a practical nurse meant that I could explain the subject to his secretary who would be traveling in the plane.

I got up in the wee hours of the dawn and proceeded to Alto Molócuè, using the African road that we had improved and crossing the Lice River over the bridge we had built. The plane arrived at ten. The president's secretary handed me a package, and I gave him another with the samples to be sent to South Africa. We sat in my car while I explained in every detail what had happened. When I finished we walked to the waiting plane. I asked, "What is in the package you gave me?"

"I do not know. It must be the medicine you asked Number One to send you. He just said to give it to you, and that he was sure you would appreciate it."

After the plane took off, I opened the package. It contained fresh apples, grapes and pears, which I certainly appreciated after eating local fruits for months.

From then on, I visited the Namivo pegmatite, which we named after the swamp, once a week. The trench was progressing fast up the side of the hill, and large chunks of beryl were constantly being found and neatly piled on the side of the trench for inspection. I had learned to tell the unusual-looking mineral apart from normal quartz and had no doubt any longer that it was in fact, beryl.

Five Achirima workers dislodge a heavy piece of beryl from the bottom of the first prospecting trench at the Namivo Mine. The trench had just reached the top of the hill. By the side of the trench, are two piles of beryl pieces (foreground and far right). Photo by the author.

The South African laboratory sent the assay results twenty days after the samples had been sent. "Their report read: 'Beryl containing 11.5% BeO,'" our company president announced over the radio, in plain language. He was so happy he could not care less whether the official listeners decided to fine him for talking business over his amateur set. "When can I visit it?" he asked.

"Any time you want," I answered.

"I'll land in Alto Molócuè the day after tomorrow."

"And, I will meet you there."

In the meantime, to protect the men from the danger of crocodiles, Nunes had built a narrow walkway of bamboo resting on green timber pegs driven into the mud of the swamp. It was not a very elegant structure. It sagged in places, but quite adequately served its intended purpose of getting you across the swamp with dry shoes, and frustrating the crocs that could neither get on it nor snap at you.

The president visited all the places where we had exposed the ridge of beryl. It formed a veritable wall that was now exposed for nearly fifty meters, and it had an average width of nearly ten meters. I showed him the map our surveyor had already prepared and indicated where I intended to cut a ditch. My plan was to lower the water level enough to drain the shallower ford, which would allow us to build a road.

At the time, I was not sure whether it would be economically feasible to drain the swamp completely. Later, when we dug a canal to let water out of the swamp, we found a dike of basic rock holding up the flow of the water. When we blasted through it with dynamite, the swamp dried up almost completely and very quickly, causing an ungainly exodus of crocodiles that climbed over each other as they raced downstream in the direction of the Molócuè River.

As soon as the swamp became dry, we built a road to the pegmatite. Next, I ordered that all bushes which might shelter mosquitoes be removed from within a radius of one kilometer. All remaining puddles of water were treated with a film of oil to suffocate mosquito larvae.

A village with quarters for the mine personnel was planned. It included a first-aid station, a central market, sports field, covered space in which food supplies could be stored, and a schoolhouse for the children of the workers. The surrounding area of ground was planted with fruit trees; we chose varieties that bear fruit rapidly, including bananas, guavas, papayas, oranges, lemons, grapefruits, tangerines, mangos and cashews. Outside this ring there was cleared land, ready to be used by the families of the workers. There they would grow their traditional crops: corn, sweet potatoes, pineapples, manioc, beans, peanuts, rice and pumpkins. The mining compound had a house for the mine superintendent, warehouses for mining equipment and supplies, maintenance shops, a fuels depot, an explosives magazine, and a large water reservoir.

I chose Zacarias (who had done an excellent job of developing the Malolo Mine), to be the superintendent at Namivo. Nunes, who was not a mining man, returned to his job of prospecting after he completed the main exploration trench.

There were no villages located near the swamp at the time we started the mining operations. The area was in Chief Gilé's jurisdiction, and I went to pay him a visit during which I explained our plans to exploit the mineral deposit and establish living facilities for workers. All aspects of the operation were explained, and I answered all his questions (as well as those of his *samassoah* and *cabo de terras*).

I especially made it clear that the mine might come to employ over one hundred workers and that we would prefer to employ local labor. We would do everything possible to make the workers' stay permanent, which was why we had cleared land for them to cultivate and planted fruit trees for their benefit.

"I will avoid bringing outsiders to your chiefdom and I know that Gilés and Ligonhas do not love each other," I said. "But it will help a lot if you explain to your people that, if they do not come to work in the mine, I will have to recruit outsiders. Also, if there are vacancies at the mine that have not been filled by Gilés and if Ligonhas from across the river want to fill them, we will not discriminate against them, or against anybody."

I knew that this argument carried a lot of weight. Indeed, in less than a week after my talk with the Gilé traditional powers, people started coming to inquire about jobs. At first, there were only a few single men. Zacarias went with them to the areas we were clearing, and explained that they could choose where they wanted to build their houses and that they would be earning money right away. Each man could have one week to build his house, and the company would pay for a crew of four workers to help him and would make tools available. The houses would be of traditional construction which was familiar to the locals and could easily be built in a week by a small crew—a bamboo frame at which balls of mud were thrown by hand to make the walls, with a roof made of bundles of cut grass overlapping each other.

The Namivo pegmatite in the early stages of development. The first two benches can be seen in the top half of the photo, and the third bench is being started in the foreground. On the right, mine cars have been loaded with beryl. Photo by the author.

The Namivo pegmatite, illustrating how the mine developed below the original level of the swamp. The area had to be kept dry by pumping out the infiltrated waters from the surrounding swampy ground (water has pooled in the foreground). At left, a group of workers is sorting the beryl and loading it into mine cars. The beryl has been blasted free from the beryl zone; this zone was probably the richest concentration ever found. Photo by the author.

As soon as workers signed up they got a blue denim shirt with a large, embroidered red "M" on it; a pair of shorts of the same material; a straw hat; a thick blanket; a set of cooking utensils; and enameled plates, mugs, forks, knives and spoons for two people. An enameled washbasin, two water buckets, and a small mirror completed the outfit. The daily ration that would be given to each worker consisted of corn or manioc flour, dried beans, dried peanuts, dried meat or fish, cooking oil, salt, sugar, coffee, and fruits in season. Families with children would receive powdered milk.

After word got around that, indeed they got to choose where they wanted their houses, and there was land already cleared where they could plant their *shambas*,[20] whole families started to come with the applicants. They would ask to see which plots were still available, would inspect them carefully, and then would choose one after long confabulations amongst all members of the family. Then, they would all sit on the ground in a circle and wait while the head of the family went to sign up. When he returned, wearing his new clothes and loaded with the other gifts, these were passed around the circle and minutely inspected by every member.

During the initial months of operation at Namivo the mining plan consisted of cutting a series of benches about twenty feet high which advanced into the hillside, parallel to the longest axis of the elliptically-shaped hill. As soon as the front of one bench reached the height of twenty feet, a new bench was started. All the benches advanced together, and all the materials produced were brought down along an inclined passageway. After about one year's time the hill had disappeared, and the pegmatite (with its concentric zones forming an ellipse that was nearly twice as long as it was wide) was completely exposed. The beryl zone was wide and extensive. There was also a fair amount of aquamarine of very good quality.

Both the use of heavy excavating and loading equipment, as well as blasting by means of explosives, are methods that have to be employed with considerable care when mining mineralized pegmatites. No two pegmatite deposits in the area resembled each other in composition. Some were massive and had their mineralization more or less contained in well-defined zones. These could be exploited by blasting with conventional explosives, and the broken material could be loaded using excavators. But the most common type of pegmatite found in the Zambezia district of Mozambique, in the center of which the Monteminas concession was located, was the zoned type where the valuable minerals were found in concentric zones resembling the layers of an onion. Every zone varied in length and thickness, and in the assemblages of different minerals. It was also common to find gems of very high value in many of the zones; and, where gems occur, rare mineral specimens are also found. These can sometimes be worth hundreds of thousands of dollars to collectors.

In fact the Namivo mine produced aquamarine that ranged from a light blue color to an intense blue that brought, in the rough state, prices above $1,000 per kilogram. The mine also produced morganite of a very delicate rose color, which was valued at about two-thirds the cost of aquamarine.

Therefore, the use of high-powered explosives or heavy-duty excavators and loaders would have been counter-productive, because both methods are quite efficient at crushing gems and damaging priceless specimens. We could not afford using conventional explosives, such as those of the nitro-glycerin family (usually called dynamites), which are generally employed in mining operations. Instead, we pioneered the use in East Africa of a hand-mixed combination of an agricultural fertilizer (ammonium nitrate) with diesel fuel, which had the very important characteristic of allowing careful breaking of the beryl gems into pieces that were not excessively small. Then the pieces could be sorted by hand.

The members of the Achirima-Lomwe tribes are a very observant people, and have a natural ability to separate minerals (even those such as quartz and beryl that look almost identical). We took full advantage of this unusual gift by training small groups of Achirima tribesmen who accompanied the mining operations, picking up any loose stones that they found among the broken rubble. Others sat on both sides of the conveyor belts that transported concentrates including quartz gems, aquamarine, morganite and crystallized specimens of columbite, tantalite and mangano-tantalite, removing any valuable specimens that came within their field of vision.

As the mining operations proceeded along the beryl-rich zones, various large pieces of a light-blue beryl were exposed on the footwall[21] of the beryl-rich zone in the second level of the mine. There was also a considerable amount of gemmy pieces of aquamarine. Because this material was different from the general mine run, Zacarias separated it and put it into bags for me to examine.

During my next visit to the mine, I was taken to the spot where the large pieces of aquamarine had appeared. After careful examination, I came to the conclusion that they were large crystals of beryl growing close to each other, whose tops had been blasted away. The beryl that Zacarias had put into bags came from that cluster of crystals. I suspected that we were mining one of the largest concentrations of beryl ever encountered. I had the bags weighed, and they weighed close to twenty tons. The gemmy material sorted by workers trained for the task was later sold to buyers from Idar Oberstein, the German gem-cutting center.

I instructed Zacarias to keep a close eye on the advancing face in order to try and expose the suspected large crystals of beryl (if in fact they existed). I also told him to keep all the beryl from these crystals separated so that we might estimate the weight and size of the crystals. A few weeks later, a runner on a bicycle brought me a message saying that a few large crystals had been exposed and that I should come to see them.

Zacarias, six feet in height, stands near a cluster of massive beryl crystals to give scale to the photo. Because there is very little color contrast between the light blue beryl and the intensely white surroundings, I outlined the beryl crystals with dashed lines. The large crystal on the left continued down into the ground and was exposed again in the next level, eight feet below. The total weight of beryl produced from this cluster of crystals exceeded ninety tons. Photo by the author.

Zacarias stands in front of two massive beryl crystals, outlined with dashes, in the pla-gioclast-spodumene-quartz-lepidolite-beryl-muscovite zone. The dark vertical lines are drill holes which were loaded with an ammonium nitrate-fuel mixture for precise blasting. Photo by the author.

Ferrotantalite started to appear on the fourth level (below the level of the original bottom of the swamp), and gradually increased in quantity until the mine's production reached over three tons per month. This was a considerable amount of a very rare mineral with a high monetary value.

The other rare compounds of the columbite-tantalite series also started to appear at depths below the fifth level, accompanied by bismuthite and native bismuth. There were also a few occurrences of cassiterite (a mineral of tin), in isolated pockets of less than ten kilos each.

The mine produced steadily for over four years, but as it went deeper the zones shrank in size and appeared in the mine's plans as smaller ellipses. The size of the beryl pieces became smaller, the amount of sheet mica increased considerably, the feldspars were less kaolinized, and it became possible to start selling large tonnages of feldspar to ceramic plants as far south as Lourenço Marques, Quelimane, and South Africa. At the same time it also became progressively more expensive to run the mine, because we had to resort to blasting more often, and increasing amounts of water had to be pumped out, day and night. In 1962, we were nearing the break-even point, at which costs would be equal to revenues. After discussing the situation with the president of the company, I gave orders to clean the pit of any traces of oils and of explosives, and then we let it flood.

The personnel had already been gradually reduced. The ones who wanted to work in our other mines, were transferred. The ones whose families had planted large *shambas* stayed around the mine, living off their cultivated fields. Because the pit had been cleaned, it was possible to successfully introduce fresh-water native varieties of fish (especially of the *tilapia* family, which are very fast growing) and the fish soon became another source of food for the people living nearby.[22]

CHAPTER EIGHT

Recruiting Laborers

During the time that we were active in the Monteminas concession, we worked about 700 pegmatites and had as many as twenty-two different mines in operation at one time. Obtaining equipment and supplies from outside the immediate area was a major ordeal; maintaining machinery in working order was also extremely challenging. Besides the natural impediments of our remote geography, the terrain, and the weather, we faced many bureaucratic obstacles as well. Nothing was easy, whether obtaining import licenses for equipment, currency permits to pay for imports, export licenses for our products, or transporting equipment, fuel, and spare parts to our sites. As a result, mechanical equipment was used as little as possible, and we relied heavily on African labor. At the peak, as many as 2,000 Africans were employed in the mines in different capacities, from skilled to unskilled.

With new mines starting production all over the area of the concession, we soon exhausted the labor reserves of the tribes in the immediate vicinity. I established the policy of giving preference to members of the tribe in whose territory each mine was located. But the tribes were small, and before our arrival in the region their men had already been in the habit of working at the large tea and coffee plantations situated to the west of us, both in Mozambique and in Malawi.

Soon we were forced to recruit from villages that were farther away, especially from the tribal groups that were settled beyond the northern limit of the concession. This option had a very serious drawback: although the villages belonged to the same basic ethnic group (the Achirima-Lomwe), spoke the same language, and had basically the same culture, they sometimes turned out to belong to different clans. Between these there might exist ancient rivalries, and you never knew when a fight would start for no apparent reason. These fights could even close down the operations of a given mine until, at my insistence, the traditional chiefs of both belligerents would hold meetings to smooth out the real or imagined disagreements and re-establish peace once again.

The *chefe de posto* of Gilé had set aside the first Friday of each month for interviews between employers and prospective employees who were members of the Lomwe and Achirima tribes residing in his area. The established meeting place was an area of swept ground around his office building, and he was available to act as referee in case there were disputes.

On a certain Friday, we sent a representative who carried a letter addressed to the *chefe de posto*, as well as written authorization to contract workers on behalf of our company. Our man returned late that night without any laborers. He told me that representatives of the tea and coffee plantations in the area of Gurué had set up tables with soft drinks and record players blaring loud music, to attract prospective workers. The plantation representatives had promised bottles of some sweet beverage as an enticement to those men who would ink their thumbs and press them onto a contract form (few of them could read). The handful of prospective workers who had come near our truck were immediately surrounded by the agents of the planters and led away towards their tables, while our man and his driver had been threatened with beatings if they interfered.

I conferred with our president, and we agreed on a plan to meet the threats that had been made and exercise our right to compete fairly in the task of recruiting laborers. When the recruitment date arrived one month later, we sent the same pickup truck as before. Again, it was loaded with clothes and blankets for distribution to any laborers who chose to work for us. But this time, we had stretched wires on the back of the truck so that the recruiter could hang up the brightly colored blankets and clothing: blue denim shirts, each with a large, bright red "M" embroidered on the back; blue denim shorts; multicolored T-shirts; and straw hats, also decorated with a bright red "M" on one side.

The pickup truck was followed by two ten-ton ore trucks, polished to a high shine. One truck carried tables and chairs, loudspeakers playing the latest popular tunes of African music, and two dozen of our strongest-built employees. Each man was dressed in blue denim with a bright red "M" on his shirt. And, they all twirled strong walking sticks.

The trucks parked and took up one side of the field used for the meeting. The tables were set on the ground, and loaded with bars of scented soap, combs, mirrors, packages of biscuits, and one-pound sacks of sugar and salt. The vehicles were immediately surrounded by curious onlookers, who were told they could choose gifts to take home to their wives and sweethearts, without any obligation to sign anything. At the same time, our strongmen walked behind the crowd, facing the competition and showing them their hefty walking sticks.

The second ore truck carried medical facilities which were set up under a tree. As soon as a man decided to sign with us, he was directed to this medical unit. There he undressed, was given a linen sack to store his clothes in, and proceeded, totally naked—in Africa, naked men do not cause raised eyebrows—to our nurse, who conducted a physical examination. Afterwards, he received his blue denim uniform and could strut around showing it off.

The trucks returned to our headquarters at Napido, full of workers.

The representatives of the competition complained loudly to our man-in-charge about the way we had carried out the operation. They were met politely and told to come to Napido to present their grievances to me. Only a few came. I listened to them, offered them a cold beer, and suggested that they put their complaints in writing and post them to His Excellency the Governor General of Mozambique. I knew that writing letters was not their forte!

After a few uneasy months passed, the problem solved itself. Most of the men we had hired worked their six-month contracts, and then came to settle with their families near the mines. We encouraged this by helping them clear enough land to establish their *shambas*. After that, we only occasionally needed to recruit personnel by attending the Gilé meetings.[23]

CHAPTER NINE

The Last Bridge

All the production from the many operating mines in the concession was transported to Napido for grading and preparation for export. The road that we used to send our mineral shipments to the port of Pebane went through a desertic region that was very rough. There were no villages, nor any trace of water in the rare river tributaries that it crossed. We used heavy Mercedes Benz trucks that made three trips a week each to the port, loaded with bags of ore for export. They returned with supplies needed in our base camp or at the various mines, such as fresh foods, mail, medical supplies; you name it.

I dreaded the possibility of an accident occurring in the stretch that was uninhabited. At the time, terrorism, which later became one of my constant concerns, had not yet become a factor in our daily life. If an accident or a breakdown occurred, the driver would have to wait at the scene until another of our trucks came by to give him assistance. Nobody else was using that road, and in those days, radio communication from the truck drivers back to their base was not possible.

A better road existed, that connected a tantalite mine to the same Pebane port on the Indian Ocean coast where all our minerals embarked for export to the United States. But the tantalite mine was on the right bank of the Melela River, while our concession and all the mines we had in production, were on the left bank. There was no bridge spanning the river.

The Melela was very wide, and the outlay of capital necessary for building a bridge did not seem justified. Nor could we expect that the government would, at least within a foreseeable or reasonable period of time, take up such an enterprise at their expense.

An alternative solution to the problem would be to build a pontoon.[24] I did some calculations and concluded that the construction and maintenance of a pontoon large enough to carry ten-ton trucks would also be very costly. So this alternative was not a very satisfactory one. The more I thought about the problem, the clearer the answer became: I had to build one more bridge. No big deal for a geologist who had already built more bridges than most civil engineers had! The key, of course, was to find a place where the Melela was narrower.

So I paid a visit to my neighbor, Chief Napido, whose village was only a few kilometers from our camp. After we concluded the polite preliminaries about the health of his numerous wives and children, the condition of his herds of scrawny goats, and the forecasts for the amount of rain to be expected during the approaching rainy season (recently "published" by the witch doctor), I broached the subject.

"I have a recollection that when we first met, you very kindly explained to me that there was an ancient African road that started at the old Morrua Fort and went through many villages belonging to many different *muénes*, and then reached Mocubela."

He nodded his head, and I continued, "So, that road must have crossed the Melela River, and I know that the Old People would not make use of roads that crossed rivers which were too deep, or too wide.

"After doing much thinking about what you told me then, I have reached the conclusion that I must visit the spot where this ancient highway crossed the Melela. Not only because I deeply admire the extraordinary feats of the Old People, but also because it might be the most appropriate place to build a bridge, so that we could send our loaded trucks in that direction. If they had chosen, as was their custom, a good crossing place, we could, then, connect to the road that goes from the tantalite mine to Mocubela. I hear that this road is very good, and actually is shorter than the one we are now using.

"Could you indicate one of your subjects that I might hire as a guide to go with me to this place? I think that the Old People must have chosen to cross the Melela River where it is narrower, but still not too deep for people to wade across."

He answered, "Certainly, I go with you myself. But it is a bit far both from here and also from your camp. And it is bad area, overgrown with thorn bushes and lots of crazy beans. Also, my goat herders never go in that area because they have met lions.

"Best way is, I think, for you to wait a few days while I send for my *cassa-cassa* and put them to clearing the track. Then we can drive in your car."

"*Orrera sano* (very well)," I agreed. "Many thanks, for your assistance in solving this very difficult but very important problem. I will be very happy to wait until the track is made good for my car to drive on it.

"And, incidentally, I would like to talk with you about *cassa-cassa* work. If I decide to build the bridge, I am going to need more laborers than I can recruit. Would it be possible for me to pay you, in cash, for your *cassa-cassa* if they come and work for me while building this bridge? Would this be legal according to your customs, and would they cooperate if we did that?"

"Trouble with *cassa-cassa* work," he answered, "is that it is only for one week. By the time they have learned the job, the week is over. Let me talk to the *cabo de terras* to find out how many men owe me more than two weeks. These will have to stay longer than the usual one week, and if you offer them good clothes, and a good salary, to work on the construction of the bridge, then after they finish their *cassa-cassa*, they may stay to the end. I find out and then I go talk to you. As for their cooperation with you, usually there is no trouble.

"They understand that working one week every year for the chief is the same as what the chief does for them—I work all year at solving their problems, to protect their interests against outsiders that want to take advantage of them. If I tell them to go do their *cassa-cassa* building a bridge, instead of working in my field of manioc, it makes no difference to them. Differences might develop from how good you feed them, how good are the blankets you give them.

"Even not receiving the money themselves is not so important, because, if they were doing their *cassa-cassa* work for me, they would not get any clothes. If they work for you and they get good clothes, they will be very happy."

He showed up at my office two weeks later, and said, "I have more than one hundred men who owe me more than two weeks of *cassa-cassa*. But we have to use them before manioc planting season starts. Also, I come to tell you, we might go see where the African road crosses the Melela. My men have cleared the track."

I drove with him to the ruins of the military post that had been abandoned before the beginning of the Twentieth Century. As he had mentioned, it was bad country, covered with tangled second-growth vegetation, creepers and thorn bushes. This was the perfect living environment for poisonous snakes, scorpions, poisonous centipedes, man-eating rogue lions, and the spirits of ancient warriors who had died here, fighting to get rid of their shackles. Or, fighting to keep their slaves in shackles!

The walls of one large building were still standing. Some smaller buildings were completely destroyed and obliterated by weeds and creepers. Napido's men had not made any attempt to clear the bushes and vines that grew over the ruins of the old fort, and it was impossible to see where the old trail had been located.

"We will not find any sign of the old road inside the grounds of the fort," said Napido. "My people believe that the fort is haunted. When they use the old African road, they make a wide detour around the ruins. We will not waste time looking for it because I know where the road crossed the Melela; there is a ford there. When I was a young man, we used to follow the old road in large groups, carrying *cangarras*[25] filled with cotton to the market in Mulevala. In those days, there were no stores or markets to the north of Mulevala. We had to walk two days to get our goods to market in the southerly direction. We can take the car close. Then we will walk to where the ford is."

We drove some distance upstream until the track got very rocky and I had to park the car. From there we walked to the river, then followed along its left bank for a couple of miles. Finally we came to a place where the Melela divided itself into a number of channels, none too wide, that flowed swiftly through narrow gaps that separated very rocky, small islands.

I had the impression that it would not be very difficult to build a series of small bridges connecting the various islands. Instead of building one large bridge, it seemed I was going to have to build various smaller ones over these narrow channels.

"Is there any hardwood timber we can use for beams and cross pieces?" I asked.

Napido shook his head. "Not here. But a few kilometers upstream there is taller forest, where you can get good timber. The difficult part is you will have to clear a road through heavily timbered terrain with many deep ravines, so you can use a big truck to bring big logs and store them here."

Up to this point the chief had been very informative and eager to cooperate, but now he became reluctant to give me more than vague information about where exactly the timber was. I had the impression that he thought he had already talked too much. I suspected that decisions about who was permitted to cut timber for the needs of the tribe came under the jurisdiction of the *cabos de terras*. Chief Napido would have to consult with the other members of the triumvirate before any more information would be forthcoming.

I decided not to force the issue. I thanked Chief Napido for his valuable help and goodwill, delivered him back to his village, and returned to our camp. There I collected the surveyor, and drove with him to the site of the rapids that I had just visited. We parked the car in the same place I had used before and walked slowly along the left bank of the Melela River. We took in every detail of the distribution channels that funneled the water through the various narrow chutes separating the rocky islands.

When we returned to the car, I told the surveyor to study the area thoroughly and try to find the most likely site to build a bridge.

"What I have in mind is, for example, to bridge this channel between the bank where we are standing, and the island in front of us. As soon as it is possible for us to drive over this first short bridge and reach the island, we will move the air compressor and use it to power the jackhammers. We will drill as many holes as necessary and then blast off the top of the island, making it flat and level with the first bridge. Then we will use the flattened surface as a roadbed across the island. From there we will build another short bridge to the next island, and repeat the procedure until we reach the right bank of the river. Naturally, at times of flooding the channels will not be capable of handling all the added flow and the river will go over our bridges. But even if we have to wait a few days to cross over, we will still be much better off than we are now. How long will it take you to prepare a map with enough points and elevations to allow us to select the best route?"

"Shouldn't take more than a few days," replied the surveyor.

One week later, I sent the completed plans to the president of our company for his approval. Within a few days, he mentioned during the early morning radio call that he was surprised to see that, *"The passageway to your radio-shack will be so easy to build. You should start it right away."*

We started on the preliminaries by building a more direct and better road from our camp to the site of construction. We also began cleaning up the bush around the site in order to build a camp for the workers; and, we built a foundation for the air compressor, carpentry and blacksmith shops, and a storage building for cement and dynamite.

Meanwhile, I made another visit to Chief Napido and, after the usual exchange of chitchat, brought up the subject of the timber for the bridge.

The chief said, "Our conversations about the construction of a bridge over the Melela River and your needs of personnel and timber were not forgotten. I gave much thinking to it and discussed it with my advisors. Your request for information on where to find timber for building the Melela Bridge has been much discussed, also. We are in agreement that this bridge will make it much easier for our people to take their cotton to the market. This is a matter that falls under the authority of the *samassoah*. He will go with you to the site and discuss with you every aspect of it, for although I am the *muéne*, it will be the *samassoah* who is responsible to the people for this very important enterprise."

The next morning I drove to the *samassoah's* village, to go in his company to see the area where the chief had said there was suitable timber. We drove a few miles along the road to Malolo, parked the Beetle, and walked in the forest towards the banks of the Melela.

The vegetation became thicker, and the trees became taller. As we approached the river, I saw that the hardwood trees became more numerous. The vegetation covering the area where our concession was located, was what is called *park forest* because the trees were widely spaced apart and of many different species. The spaces in between them were occupied by tall grass and abundant bushes. Here and there might be patches where one species abounds and stifles others. Especially in deep valleys, there may exist large concentrations of one kind of tree.

After leaving the car, we walked for quite a distance through a beautiful and peaceful open forest with many flowering bushes. The ground sloped gently to the south, and there were no rocks underfoot, nor creepers to tackle you around the knees and make you fall.

Finally, the *samassoah* pointed to a narrow gully where straight, tall trees with thick trunks were visible above the surrounding screen of bushes.

"Those *muihree* (trees) are the ones Chief Napido was talking about. We do not tell outsiders about them. He should not have told you before he had listened to his advisors.

But the bridge you want to build is very important to take our cotton to market. We are all very excited about this news that you might really build it, and we already know that you are capable and know how to build bridges because we also see that the other bridge you build, over the river Lice, has been covered by waters during a flood and it was not carried away by the waters. And it is now much easier for our people to travel to Chief Novanana's village.

"Because Novanana is our Paramount Chief and we all go there at certain times of the year, we know these things. We also know that Novanana is good friend of yours. In the past, when we visit our Paramount Chief, we sometimes had to camp and wait a few days to cross the Lice when the water was high.

"This is why we agree to tell you where the hardwood trees are. Please, you promise me to only cut trees you need for bridge. No more. And, please, you tell no one else where they are.

"We, the Elders, like to learn new things that make the people live better than they did before. The young people, they want to have money and to be able to buy all kinds of new things. Some of these things are good. But lots of them are only good for making you work more for things that are useless. We are sad to see many things disappear completely from our beautiful Africa, like these trees. These trees cry when people cut them!"

This speech, which was delivered in a self-conscious and almost embarrassed way, did not touch on any matters that I did not already know. But it underscored the responsibility that rests on the shoulders of anyone who uses "progressive" or "modern" methods without giving serious consideration to the conservative and delicately-balanced environment of Old Africa.

I reconnoitered the gully thoroughly, and concluded that there was more than enough timber. Most of the trees had thick enough trunks, and grew straight for more than six meters. But I immediately noticed one problem, which looked very difficult to solve. How would we transport the timber to the bridge site? Of course this was not the *samassoah's* concern, and I did not discuss it with him. On the way back to camp I kept running over and over in my head various ways to tackle the problem, but without finding a solution.

That evening in my office, I interviewed an applicant for a job. He was a miner whom I had trained in the art of timbering underground tunnels while I had been director of the Alto Ligonha Mines. He had worked in the construction of the tunnels that I had driven under the Muiane and Naípa mines, that were used for hauling broken rock from the various levels of those mines. He was just the right man needed for the bridge job, where I intended to use heavy pieces of timber as platforms on which vehicles would roll.

During the conversation that followed, I mentioned the difficulty I was fore-seeing in getting the timber out of the ravine where the trees were growing, and the expected difficulties of transporting it to the site of the proposed bridge. He suggested that, instead of trying to drag the heavy logs up to a road, we could roll the logs down to the river and then float them on the river to the bridge site.

"Brilliant idea!" I said, "but I foresee one very serious problem with it. This kind of wood does not float. It is not only green, but also so dense that, even if it were dry, it would sink in water."

The surveyor, who was also present at the meeting, spoke up. "If that is the only problem that we will face, do not worry about it. I will make those logs float. We will cut the trees, and clean them of branches and square them at the site where they are felled. This will lighten their weight. Then we can drag them down to the river, sliding them over rollers and pulling by hand-cranked winches. I'll attach enough empty oil drums to each individual log, tied to rope slings in pairs, so that they will float! Then, we will 'sail' them all the way to the bridge using paddlers on top of each log. They will paddle down the river, using their paddles to hit vigorously any crocodiles that get tempted to approach too closely!"

The idea of "sailing" the timber logs to the site, especially the suggestion that the paddlers could hit the crocs over the head whenever they came too close, made me laugh. But after I gave it more thought, it sounded reasonable.

Soon, nearly one hundred men arrived to begin work. They were a ragged-looking crowd (for no *cassa-cassa* who has any sense will report to work wearing good clothes).

They were shown to the camp we had prepared for them. After they had set-tled down and had been served an abundant meal, I talked to them, using their leader as interpreter. It went something like this.

"I see all of you, and I greet you. You all know who I am, and you know that you are here to help me build a *rampahn*.[26] This *rampahn* is very important, because it will make it easier for me to send trucks loaded with minerals to the port of Pebane, so that the minerals can be put into the big ships. The minerals will be taken over the sea so that the *Miricani*[27] can buy them. That is a very important reason to build the *rampahn*. But another reason is that it will make transportation of your cotton to market much cheaper."

I made an extended pause, to give them a chance to digest such a large collection of new ideas.

"So, it is right that we should work together. But 'work together' does not mean that you will work *de mahala* (for nothing). The *cassa-cassa* work you owe to Chief Napido, you will do for me instead, and I will pay him in cash. You will be discharged of the debt of *cassa-cassa* you owe to your chief."

Here I made another long pause, because this new idea of transferring *cassa-cassa* liabilities from one party to another was one that I considered rather risky and precedent-making. Therefore, lots of time had to be allowed for it to sink in.

"To you," I continued, "I will give good food, and plenty of it. We will also give every man a pair of shorts, a shirt and one blanket. At the end of your *cassa-cassa* work, we will give you a gift of food to take home with you, for your families.

"If you want to stay after you have completed your *cassa-cassa,* I will give you the same salary as we pay the men who work in the mines, and when you learn new things, you get increases in salary, in the same way that the men who work in the mines do.

"If you want to stay even longer, after the work of building the bridge is finished you can work in the mines if you wish. It will be a new job, and you will have the right to new clothes and a new blanket.

"I hope that every man has understood what I just said. If you have not understood all, you should ask right now, and I will repeat and explain again. If, while you are working here, you have complaints to make, or if somebody has not treated you right, you must speak to me. I will be visiting the bridge site every day, and I always listen."

I waited another while, searching their faces for signs of the effect of my speech, and then continued. "But this is not the end of my talk to you, because I have not said the most important thing. Most important thing is not that you have to work well. I know you are going to work well. The Achirima are good workers! The most important thing is that we are going to build this *rampahn* without accidents. You want to get back to your villages as soon as possible to start planting *mandioca*.[28] But if you get hurt, you go to the hospital, and you will not get home in time for planting *mandioca*. So, you keep thinking: no accidents! Good luck!"

I supervised as the work progressed from drilling the holes, loading them with dynamite, and blasting off the top of the first island. Meanwhile, the new man I had just hired directed the cutting and trimming of the first two logs. Once ready, they were dragged down to the water using hand-cranked winches. Then, the logs were placed over slings of rope, which were wound around pairs of empty oil drums spaced at equal intervals and connected to each other by ropes. Each log rested on four pairs of drums. On top of each pair of drums, there was a small platform made of planks of wood, where the "sailors" sat, each with a paddle, to help the current take the logs downstream.

When the men who were busy at the bridge site glimpsed the first "raft" coming around a bend in the river, upstream from where they were, they all stopped working and many of them dropped their tools and were about to start running away towards the river bank! However, the *capataz* raised his arms and told them to stop. Then he explained that it was their own friends coming down, sitting on top of big pieces of timber.

After the first log arrived, the paddlers were received with greetings and slaps on their backs. I waited for everyone to calm down, then pointed to the upstream side of the island and told them to park the big log there and to anchor it by means of big rocks tied to ropes.

"You did a good job," I told the paddlers. "Now, you rest, for there is no more work for you today. Tomorrow you go back up and report to your boss."

I was surprised at the instinctive reaction of the men when they first saw the "raft," and asked the *capataz* what had caused the panic amongst some of the workers.

"We walk to your car, and I explain."

When we got to my parked car, out of the hearing of the workers, we sat down and he said, "There are many old legends that we, the Achirima, learn during childhood. In the evening, everybody gathers and sits around the campfires, which are lighted in the villages, and we listen to the storytellers. This is the way that the history of our tribe is taught to the children. Not only history, but also morals, customs, and traditions are taught in this way.

"Sometimes, a thing happens that revives these ancient tales, and the people act according to superstition, not according to logic. That is what happened here today.

"There are many legends that refer to the fact that, in the old days, there came from the East big ships that anchored out at the mouth of this same river where we are working (the Melela River), where it enters the sea. From those ships were lowered long canoes loaded with many soldiers armed with firearms (which the people had never heard of nor seen before). And these war canoes sailed up the Melela River, as far as they could go, and when they could not sail anymore, the soldiers disembarked and marched into the interior where our ancestors lived, and they surrounded our villages and took the people, tied by the neck to long poles, into slavery."

"You mean to say that just because those men with paddles in their hands reminded some of the workers of the canoes mentioned in an ancient legend, they thought of a slavers' raid and went into a panic? That seems very unlikely," I said.

"Yes, it seems far-fetched," answered the *capataz*. "But do not forget that we are working at a place loaded with superstition. This is where a very ancient African road crossed the river. That road was used by Arab and Indian slavers for penetrating into the interior. Do not forget also that we are just around a bend in the river from the Old Morrua Fort. The Portuguese built this fort at the site of a bloody battle where they destroyed the forces of Ibrahimo, the last important Arab slaver from Parapato (now called Angoche).

"To the Achirima, Morrua is haunted by the spirits of the ones who died in the battle, as well as of the slavers that the Portuguese hanged afterwards. The people avoid this place due to the presence of those spirits. The spirits of the dead are deeply feared by the people. They believe that the spirits of nasty individuals, and of criminals who were punished for bad deeds during their lifetime, stay around the places where they once lived. They are waiting for opportunities to take revenge for their punishment."

"You do not believe in haunted places, do you?" I asked.

"No sir, I don't. I am Achirima, but I was educated at the M'bua Mission."

The project of connecting the rocky islands in the rapids of the Melela River, near the prominent Mount Morrua and the historical ruins of the Morrua Fort, progressed at a good pace. As the work continued, I shifted my role so that I personally controlled the cutting and floating of hardwood logs to the bridge site. I had given my word to the *samassoah* of the Napido clan that we would cut no more hardwoods than were needed for the construction; therefore, the logs were cut and floated to the bridge site just as they were needed. I did not allow any stockpiling, and when the construction ended there was not one single log left over.

The man who directed the felling of the trees told me that these hardwoods emitted a sound, like a screech or a cry, when they started to fall. He thought that the strange sound "Was probably caused by the snapping of the long, hard fibers of which they are made."

I remembered then that the *samassoah* had told me not to cut more trees than I needed for the bridge because, "These trees cry when people cut them!"

Using hand tools—chisels made by the blacksmith and long-handled sledge-hammers—we chiseled embrasures into which the ends of the logs were fitted. Hand-forged rock-bolts secured the ends of the beams to their seats. On top of the main beams, we bolted crosspieces of smaller cross-section, made from a very abundant species of hardwood. The crosspieces, in their turn, supported thick planks of the same kind of timber and formed the deck of the bridge, on top of which the wheels of the vehicles would run.

After the first bridge span had been built, I left the new man in charge of the operations and returned to my duties supervising the mining and prospecting projects that were being developed. I visited the construction site once every week. The new man and the workers from Napido got on quite well, and most of the *cassa-cassa* workers stayed on after their obligation to their chief had been discharged.

Three months from the start of construction, I rode over the full length of the bridge.[29] I drove through to the connecting road on the right bank of the Melela that intersected the existing road to Mulevala. Then I went and paid a visit to our nearest neighbors at the Morrua tantalite mine.

CHAPTER TEN

Salt Jobs

The president of the company wanted me to inspect a mine located outside of the area of our concession, which had been offered to him for sale. The seller had been rather emphatic about the extent and the high grade of the mineralization that was supposed to extend over a considerable area, and to contain abundant tantalite.[30]

During the daily 5:00 a.m. radio contact, I was informed in our private coded language that the owner of the mine was to be contacted in Gilé, the administrative post where we recruited workers for our mines. Gilé is located on the right bank of the Molócuè River, the stream that was the northern limit of our concession.

When I asked the *chefe de posto* of Gilé about the man who owned the tantalite deposit, I was told that the person was not a resident. Rather he was a partner in one of the trading stores located in the village, who bought agricultural products from the natives and sold them manufactured goods. At the trading store mentioned by the *chefe de posto*, the storekeeper first said that he did not know the person I was asking about. However, when I said I had come to visit a mine that was offered for sale, he admitted knowing the man but stated that the man had nothing to do with the store and was not there. I told the storekeeper that I would return in a week's time to visit the claims and wanted the owner to be present when I made my examination of them.

A week later, I returned as promised and was met by an African who presented me with a letter from the owner of the mining claims. The letter stated that he could not come, but that "the bearer of this letter" would show me around.

We drove across the Molócuè River and then along a barely-visible track that went on and on through the featureless savanna. Eventually, I was told to stop among some low hills. We climbed up to the top of the most prominent hill, and from there the guide pointed out the corner markers of the mining claims that were for sale. It seemed that the area enclosed by the distant corner markers was, indeed, quite extensive.

Prospecting pits had been dug on a square grid about 400 meters on each side. The pits seemed to be all over the area; I walked to the nearest one, which had been sunk to a depth of nearly five meters, and looked inside it. It was evident the pit had been completed more than one year before, because I could see the effects of the last rainy season. Rain had washed the silt off the walls and cut furrows exposing small grains of tantalite embedded in a matrix of quartz fragments and deeply altered pieces of feldspar.

I checked another dozen pits, in a random fashion. Some had been located on the flanks of the hills. Others were in the shallow valleys between them, and a few were on the tops. In all of them, I observed that tantalite was present—small, tabular, dark red grains, that seemed to be distributed evenly throughout. In conclusion: it looked very good!

During the return trip, I asked the African guide if he had dug the pits. He shook his head.

Did he know who had?

Same answer.

When had the work been done?

One more shake of the head.

At the site, he had seemed to know everything about the claims offered to us for sale, but now he had become dumb! Something was making me suspicious, but I could not put my finger on what it was.

I left him at the trading store before driving back to my camp at Napido. During the long trip back, I went over in my mind all that had happened during the visit and tried unsuccessfully to pinpoint what it was that made me uneasy about the whole situation.

The next morning, the president inquired over the radio if I had already visited "his friend" in Gilé, and whether I had liked his friend's "plantation." I told him that it was quite extensive, but I avoided saying that it looked exceptionally good because I suspected the owner would be listening to our conversation. I suggested that we should get the owner's permission to re-sample the existing pits and sink a few new ones, in order to check results.

A fortnight later, the president said over the radio, "My friend from Gilé has invited you to visit his plantation. He has a crew there waiting to help you."

This evidently meant I had permission to sample the pits; otherwise, there would be no need for the crew to be "waiting to help me" at the site. No mention had been made about sinking new check-pits, and I was being offered a crew that

I had not requested and which I certainly would not trust to perform a sensitive task such as re-sampling a prospect offered for sale!

Once more I returned to the trading store at Gilé, but this time I took with me a very experienced former employee of the Geological Survey, whom I had just hired as a prospector. During the long trip I gave the prospector all the information I had, emphasizing that I felt there was something suspicious, and cautioning him to be especially alert for some kind of trickery.

The storekeeper told me that we were welcome to re-sample the pits and inspect the whole area.

"The owner does not think there is any need to sink new pits. Because it is so difficult to get laborers in that area, we have put together a crew to help you. It will be led by the *capataz* who put down the pits; the same one who went with you to show where the claims were."

I distinctly remembered this person pretending that he did not know who had put down the pits, or when it had been done!

We did not linger at the trading store, but drove to the area where the claims were. On arrival, I saw that there was a camp with newly built huts where a group of laborers was housed. The man who had guided me previously came to greet us and pointed out a place where the prospector could put up his tent. I noted that the location was one which he could keep under observation from his own camp, so I shook my head and said, "No, it is too close to the workers' camp. The prospector is the person who will choose the location he prefers for his own campsite. When he does so, then you can start to set it up the way he tells you."

I walked over the area with the prospector and explained in detail how I wanted him to do the job. I cautioned him not to trust that crew of workers, especially their *capataz*. We unloaded his gear at the place he chose for his camp, and I left.

Back at Napido, I gave more thought to the subject and decided to send my lab assistant, Pampuela, to assist the prospector. I had previously trained Pampuela to prospect for tantalite deposits in Alto Ligonha. I told him about my suspicions and said, "I want you to act like an ordinary *capataz*, not showing that you are a trained prospector. Choose six of our men that you know and trust, to go with you. It would be better if they were all Achirimas.[31] The crew that is already there is made up of Lomwes. You can pretend you do not understand their language and keep listening to their talk. If you hear anything that explains why they are acting so suspiciously, inform the prospector immediately. I want our men to work as ordinary unskilled laborers under the guidance of the prospector. I want them to play dumb; listen; watch out for anything that is not ordinary practice; and report it to you, out of the hearing of that Lomwe crew."

My instructions to the prospector had been to sample a few pits, chosen at random in each line. Samples would be taken by cutting a groove on one of the four walls of each pit. The samples would be identified with reference numbers and kept under constant observation until they were transported to our main camp. Pampuela would have the responsibility of keeping an eye on the samples, to make sure that no member of the other crew ever had a chance to introduce anything into the sample bags.

I had also instructed the prospector to sink a few new sample pits at random in between the existing lines, register their positions accurately on his map, and sample them. If the owner of the claims came to complain that he was doing unauthorized work, he was to play dumb. The samples from these pits were to be given letters instead of numbers, so that the crew at Napido would know immediately that these were "check-up samples," to be concentrated with special care. I expected that, if an attempt at inflating the value of the deposit had been made, we would find generally lower values in the pits randomly put down by our men.

We first verified in our laboratory that the samples from the pits made by the owner contained very high values of tantalite. But when the first samples from the pits sunk "randomly" by our prospector were treated, they showed extremely low values.

There was no doubt in my mind now. The pits had been "salted," and there was no need to continue wasting time and money on a worthless deposit!

Nevertheless, to make sure that I was interpreting the evidence correctly I asked the prospector to re-sample a few of the original pits. This was done by removing approximately ten inches off the surface of one wall, so as to reach an undisturbed layer, and then taking a sample off the newly-exposed wall. In every case, the results from these samples showed zero or very little tantalite.

We concluded that the salting had been accomplished in a very cunning way. The inside of the pits had been carefully plastered with a wet mixture of clay and tantalite concentrates (which had likely been stolen from one of the mines in the Alto Ligonha area). The perpetrators then let one rainy season go by, to make the "treated" walls of the pits look natural.

It was a very clever ruse that almost worked. I might have been fooled, except that my suspicions were raised by signs of unease shown by the owner of the trading store, and because the real owner of the claims never showed up.

To make sure that the facts were clearly presented to the president of our company, I asked over the radio to go see a doctor. To his query about what was wrong I answered, "I wish I knew." He sent a plane to pick me up, and that same evening I sat in his office and told him the whole story.

"So, is that what you mining people call a 'salt job?'"

"Yes, Number One," I answered. "A perfect and brilliant example of the ancient art of salting mines—and quite cleverly executed. It is up to you to expose their attempt to commit fraud. But it will be up to me to present the evidence, and to be quite frank, I don't relish the job."

"No," he responded, "we have already wasted enough valuable time and money. I will ask the man to call on me, close the door of my office, and tell him what I think of his morals. But we will leave it at that. Please tell those of our men who know what happened not to talk about it."

We discussed other matters and, as I got up to leave, he said, "There is another character wanting to give me some beryl claims in payment for an old debt. I will let him know that, in order to accept the claims as settlement for his debt, I will require a written evaluation from you. However, he will have to hire you himself and pay you for the job. When you have some free time, let me know. I'll tell him then to contact you."

"It will not work, Number One," I said. "If the guy pays me, I am bound to take his side. Suppose this turns out to be another 'salt job' like the one we have just finished investigating. Where will I be? If there should be any dispute later, I would have to take his side."

Some time later I was given instructions to meet a man in the area of the Mugeba administrative post, at the intersection of two roads. I drove over the new bridge we had built over the Melela River and followed the road taken by our trucks when they went to the port of Pebane. However instead of turning east at Mulevala, I continued south past the village of Mugeba and came to the intersection which would be my rendezvous. The meeting place was in the middle of nowhere, but the man was waiting for me. I followed his car for a considerable distance until we stopped at an abandoned farm.

"We have to walk from here," said the man. "There is a trail, but it is now in bad shape. I will lead and you can follow me."

We passed by a large pile of mica[32] that was covered by creepers and grass. I stopped, pushed the grass aside, and picked up a "book" of mica. I examined it and asked if it was from the beryl claim. He said yes, that the pile was made up of mica that came from the beryl pit located just around the corner.

"I piled it here because the ground is flat and close to where the beryl was being mined at that time. I was going to hire some workers to sort it, but with one thing and another, never did."

"Do you have any idea," I asked, "how many tons of mica are in that pile?"

"Not exactly, I don't, but it is well over 500 tons. If you want to measure, there are some workers in the beryl pit. I can have them clean up around the mica pile so you can take your measurements."

"That would be good."

The beryl pit was nearby. It was completely hidden by tall grass, bushes, and creepers. It was a large, elliptical pit with vertical walls nearly sixty feet high. A steep ramp cut along one side allowed access to the bottom. There were six laborers sitting down in the pit, their tools at their sides. They had finished cleaning up the bottom and had done an excellent job. Now they were sent to tidy up around the mica dump, and the owner left me and went with them.

I sat on a large rock in the middle of the abandoned pit and looked around. I could see a wide mica zone that encased an even wider zone where some large beryl crystals had been left in place. They were of a striking blue color[33] that made them easy to notice. It seemed very unlikely that whoever had been in charge of the mining operations would have forgotten to remove those crystals, which were worth a few thousand dollars. This fact suggested that the crystals could have been left in place to indicate there were still many others yet to be exposed.

On the inside of the beryl zone was a narrow zone of quartz that was the core of the pegmatite. The location and shape of the rock in the center of the pit invited a visitor to sit and examine at leisure the whole of the abandoned pit. It took me some time to realize that when you sat there, your attention was drawn to the beryl crystals that had been left in their original places. However, from that vantage point you could not see the zone of quartz.

As I looked around, the reason why the beautiful beryl crystals had been left behind suddenly became quite clear. It also became clear that the narrow zone of quartz was the clue to the reason why the mine had been put up for sale: the central zone of quartz was narrow because the pegmatite was "bottoming." In other words, it was closing like the shell of a boat closes around the keel! Whoever had supervised the mining had recognized what was happening and, before all the beryl was gone, had left a few crystals in place to give the impression that there was still lots of it left.

Pretty cunning trick, I thought. And offering a worked out claim in settlement of an old debt was also a rather smart trick.

I started to follow mentally the parts of the scheme that they had hatched out: the deed of sale would probably mention "one claim of beryl located in such and such a place, registered in the Mines Department of Mozambique under such and such a reference number, tendered in full payment of (the value of the debt)." If we accepted the claims in settlement of the old debt, and found later that there was no beryl left, we would have no legal redress because the value of the claim given in exchange for the amount owed, had been checked *in situ* by a qualified geological engineer (me!).

It was a neatly thought-out swindle. Firstly, the sale would cancel a debt that they could not or did not want to pay. Secondly, they would get rid of worked-out mining claims right before the Mines Department started to levy taxes. Those taxes would normally be collected until the completion of reclamation work that the original owners were supposed to perform, such as filling in the mined-out pit and fencing it.

Under normal conditions, I would simply have reported my conclusion from the *in situ* examination that the claims were worked out and valueless. But their attempt to fool an examining geologist by leaving a few strategically-placed, beautifully-colored, beryl crystals, plus the cunningly placed, comfortable rock to sit on and observe the crystals, had made me mad. It amounted to a sly attempt to salt the claims, and I thought they deserved to be taught a lesson.

All that mica, accumulated in the pile I had noticed, gave me an idea. If all of it turned out to be of the same quality as the piece I had examined, it would be worth more than the amount owed to our president—even considering the costs of cutting and grading it, and reclaiming the mined-out pit. So, I decided to examine the mica in detail.

I climbed out of the pit and walked to where the mica was. The workers had removed all the weeds, and I saw immediately that the tonnage was considerable. Using compass and tape, I established a square grid and proceeded to estimate the approximate tonnage of the pile. It was over two thousand tons. Next, I asked the owner to direct the workers to cut a narrow trench through the pile so that I could see if the quality of the mica was the same from top to bottom.

While they attacked it from opposite sides, I walked over the whole area of the claims. I noted the locations of the property beacons and the condition of the house, outbuildings, and the access road. At one end of the area was a stream, and I walked down toward it to see whether there was enough water running in it to support the mica-washing operation, which would precede the cutting. Before the light started to fail, I had examined the trench the laborers had cut and concluded that the accumulated mica was in good condition and of average-to-good quality. I promised the owner I would send a report to the president of our company within a week, and I left.

Instead of driving back to my camp I spent the night in Mocuba, the county seat. Mocuba was a fairly large town with a railway station, and I was able to contact the president by telephone.

I described my observations in detail. First, there were no more than a few tons of beryl present, which had been left at prominent places to give the impression that there was a lot of it. In fact the beryl zone had been worked out, and the pegmatite was "bottoming."

Second, they had accumulated a few thousand tons of rough mica in a pile located between the house and the mined-out pit, obviously intending to have it cut for export. But they had never actually started (and I suspected that they did not know how to do it). I indicated that the mica was still in good condition.

Third, within the area of the claims were an abandoned farmhouse and some outbuildings that could be repaired and used to house personnel and as cutting sheds. Sufficient running water was available to wash the mica before cutting it.

Finally, there was enough mica present to bring a return on the order of $200,000 after it was cut properly, and, among the men employed in our concession, there were enough experienced mica-cutters from which to assemble a good crew.

I told my employer that I would be reporting to him in writing within a week, and that my recommendation would be that he accept the claims in settlement of the debt, but make sure that the deed of sale mentioned only *registered mining claims*, and not *beryl claims*. This way they could not complain that they sold us *beryl*, but that we took out *mica*. My suspicions might be far-fetched, but after two attempts to fool me with "salted claims," I was not in the mood to trust my fellow (mining) men.

After the deal was completed and the claims were registered in the name of our company, I sent a crew with instructions to repair the farmhouse and build a camp for the workers. The crew also constructed a warehouse, to store the stock of raw mica out of the weather, and sheds, where our trained mica-cutters could process it. When all was ready, I sent a man with long experience in this kind of work to direct twelve mica-cutters, and the work got underway. It became a very successful and profitable operation. We processed the mica from the stockpile, as well as similar material that we bought from various local prospectors.

About a year later, the president mentioned during our early morning radio call that, "Your prophecy about our football team being accused of exporting shiny things that we had not purchased, is being fulfilled. Prepare yourself to explain our point of view to King Solomon in a couple of weeks. I will send up a kite."

Just as I had anticipated, the man who had paid his debt by tendering worked-out claims in settlement was now suing our company. He was asking for damages for invasion of property, unlawful exploitation, and illicit sale of minerals owned by him. In cases of this kind, the first action by the judge appointed to investigate the facts would be to hear the allegations made by the plaintiff's side. Then he would call the defendants and ask them to disclose the case for the defense.

We learned later that the plaintiff alleged that he had paid a debt to our president by deeding to him some claims of beryl that he owned and that, after the transfer of ownership, we had processed and sold mica that he had stockpiled in the area of one beryl claim. He also alleged that we altered a farmhouse located within the area, built a warehouse and sheds in which we processed the mica, and otherwise acted in the pursuit of profits, of which he claimed his due share.

When our lawyer was asked to present our side, he addressed the investigating judge saying that we did not deny any of the facts presented by the plaintiff.

"Our defense rests on articles of the Mining Law of Mozambique stating that the owner of a registered mining claim is entitled to the minerals mentioned on the title of the claim, as well as any other minerals found therein, as well as the timber and waters that may occur within the borders of the claim. There is also an article in the same Law that states that buildings and installations are an integral part of the mining and processing of minerals and may not be sold separately from the mining property.

"We further intend to show that the geologist who inspected the claims prior to their transfer of ownership to the defendant wrote a report in which he described that there was little beryl, but abundant mica in the property. I will submit the report as evidence. Furthermore, the author of that report is present in this court and may answer any questions Your Excellency may wish to make."

The Judge turned to me and said, "You are not under oath, and you have not been qualified as an expert witness at this time. My questions to you are only to ascertain what you may be able to contribute to this case if and when you testify under oath. Will you testify that you saw little beryl and abundant mica in the area of the claims?"

"Yes, Your Excellency, I will so testify."

"Will you testify also, that you saw and made mention in a report to your employer, a stockpile of mined mica and the existence of a house and outbuildings?"

"Yes, I will, Your Excellency," I answered.

The Judge rose and said, "This preliminary session is completed. I will notify the parties of further procedures." He left the room, and so did we.

I heard later that the investigating judge had found the plaintiff without grounds to sue, and therefore the case was dismissed.

CHAPTER ELEVEN

Building a New Kaya[34]

The bridge we had built over the Melela River on the road to Pebane was completed and opened to traffic when I returned to the Napido Camp after reporting on the salt jobs. It was now possible for cars traveling between the important district capitals of Quelimane and Nampula to save many kilometers of rough roads by using the bridge. Foreseeing that this route would become the preferred one for persons traveling between those cities, our president offered to donate the bridge to the government. As a result, we had a visit from the engineers of the Public Works Department of the Government of Mozambique, who inspected it and pronounced it safe for vehicles not exceeding twenty tons gross weight. They also showed me how to make it safe for twice that tonnage, by increasing the cross-section of the crosspieces. Because we shipped our minerals in ten-ton trucks, I considered my goal to have been achieved. If they wanted to make it safe for over twenty tons, they could do it themselves as it was their bridge now.

In my opinion, the only thing that was left for us to do was to inaugurate it with pomp and ceremony in keeping with the national impact of this "marvel of bush engineering."

I went hunting and shot three large kudu. We bought many baskets of cassava roots and countless bunches of bananas. An enormous table was assembled on one of the spans of the bridge. Chief Napido, accompanied by his *cabos de terras* and *samassoah*, plus all the inhabitants of his village and all the *cassa-cassas* and other laborers who had sweated to build the bridge, came to sit around the table and partake of kudu roasted on the coals accompanied by freshly-roasted cassava and lots of bananas.

Africans do not go in for speeches (except in court, to impress the judge). Neither do I. I simply thanked them for their cooperation on the project that was in their interest as much as it was in ours. When the food ran out, the ceremony was over. Everybody gathered the clean bones and the banana skins and threw them in the river—there was no reason to attract hyenas to the bridge, and the crocodiles might even appreciate the bones. (To this day, I am ignorant of whether they ate the banana skins as well.)

Our minerals production had become regular and Napido was the convergence point where all materials came to be packed for export. Therefore, the company decided it was time to build permanent houses there for me and the other senior employees. I drew up plans for the proposed "town." It was the first—and only—time that I engaged in city planning.

I have never had the time or the opportunity to discuss with other "town planners" what they consider to be the most important guidelines in laying out the streets and the various centers of activity of a town. Ours was built according to the parameters dictated by our unique situation. Principle among these was the remoteness of the Napido camp, which was distant from any other urban center. The camp was alternatively known as "The One Hundred and Fifty Camp," because it was 150 kilometers from Napido to Alto Molócuè, the administrative center of the county; it was also 150 kilometers to Pebane, the port through which we exported our mineral production. And, it took another 150 kilometers of driving through bush tracks to go to church at the M'bua Mission on Sundays!

Our remote location made it necessary for us to produce our own electric power. We also needed large warehouses to maintain sufficient food supplies for the workers and adequate repair shops to keep our fleet of vehicles operative. This was especially critical during the rainy season, when we could be isolated from the rest of the world for weeks at a time. We needed medical facilities capable of handling emergencies until a doctor arrived. We could call the doctor in Alto Molócuè by radio, and he never failed to come in response to our summons. However, it would take him two to four hours to reach us depending on whether the road was dry or covered with mud.

There were other imperatives that had to be treated with respect and obeyed. One was the climate, which was sub-tropical with two long seasons: one dry and cool, and the other very wet and hot. Another was the need to watch costs very carefully: we produced a few rare minerals that had to be transported great distances to reach their markets, drastically reducing our margins of profit. Both of these factors were of paramount importance.

There were also favorable conditions that we could use to our advantage, in order to offset the unfavorable ones. We were surrounded by forests that were abundant with good timber, which could be used as a source of lumber. By submitting a written request indicating the reasons for the use of the timber, government permission could be obtained to cut a stipulated number of trees for

non-commercial purposes. Another advantage was that among the African population were many artisans interested in earning salaries for working at their trades.

All of these facts, in addition to the buildings already in place, guided my
"town planning" and were taken into consideration.

When we first had arrived in the Napido area, I had inquired of Chief Napido
where he thought the best place for me to establish our camp would be. He, in
turn, handed the decision to his *samassoah* who took me to an open, fairly flat
area, covered with grass but with very few bushes where mosquitoes could hide
during the day (and come out to feed on us at night). Therefore, in retrospect I
realized that I had accepted the *samassoah's* idea of a likely place to settle down
strictly on the dictates of anti-malarial considerations.

I remembered that I chose the place where my tent was originally set up, and
which became the VIP part of Napido Town later, because there were three tall
trees that would contribute the air conditioning necessary for me to sleep com-
fortably during the rainy season and would act as a barrier to the cold winds of
the dry season. The place was at the edge of the small plateau, and it had a good
view. Therefore, the criterion for that choice had been an aesthetic one.

At some point during those first three years, the pre-fabs had arrived. The first
pre-fabricated building that housed the office and the lab was built where the trail
ended and where it was most convenient for the trucks to unload the building
materials. It was also located in the center of the area that was now under consideration to become "Napido Town" and was about to lose the title of "Camp."
When I had been "promoted" to a pre-fab, made of composite-board slabs
mounted on top of concrete-filled gasoline cans, I had donated my canvas tent to
two new employees. I chose to locate my new residence on the other side of the
office, so as to be as far away as possible from the men's noisy portable radios. In
this case, the operating criterion was a selfish desire for peace and quiet.

Other edifices had been built as the need for them arose. We already had a
large building that housed the minerals treatment plant, as well as a rudimentary
hospital and car maintenance facility. We had also built a shack for the electric
generator and warehouses to store foodstuffs for the workers, and they had been
positioned according to a concept that I had developed in my mind and which
would not interfere with the overall site plans that were to be submitted to the
company's head office.

I had decided that the main street would be a wide avenue passing in front of
the office building and ending in front of my house. There would be another res-
idential street, at right angles to Main Street, and it would end at the surveyor's
house. But when I showed the plan to the surveyor, he immediately found fault
with it, saying, "No sir, we cannot place my future residence there!"

"And why not?" I asked. "It is an airy place. You would be away from the noise and activity that goes on near the office and the maintenance shops, and far enough away from the nearest other residents."

"It is all that you say. You are right in those respects, and I do not deny them. But don't you remember that when we had our tents set up under those big trees at the end of the camp, a lion walked between your tent and mine?"

"I remember quite distinctly that I was doubtful of the presence of any lion, until you pointed out to me the impressions of its pug marks on the dust. It was a heavy male, still young because its footprints were very distinct and flawless. But I have assumed that you would realize that a lion which walks between two flimsy canvas tents (that could be torn to pieces if he took just one swipe at them) and doesn't harm us, would certainly not attempt to attack a solid house!"

The surveyor continued his remarks, unimpressed by my logic. "And, I am sure you remember that recently the night watchmen had to go and hide inside the office building because there was a lion walking in the moonlight, right down the main street of the camp. That lion has been seen cutting across the camp at night, and he always walks between where we first camped and the place where you want my house to be built. When the street that ends at this place is finished, it will offer him an open, smooth highway to walk directly to my house! And I don't like that!"

Obviously, he had not recovered from a near encounter with a lion that occurred while we were working together at another location.[35] So, I moved his future house to a different position closer to the main street.

Armed with all the above parameters, I "went to town" and applied them to the production of the master plan on which the future development of Napido Town would rest. I sent the plans to headquarters, and they were approved. The president indicated that a clinic and my house should be built first. We started looking for brick-makers, stone masons, carpenters and other artisans among the village dwellers inside the area of the concession, and even as far north as Gilé and as far south as Mocubela. With the help of both Chief Novanana and Chief Napido, suitable crews were found and put under contract. I checked all the information available from the natives about where suitable building materials existed, with a view to gathering as many materials as needed without having to pay the heavy costs of transportation.

At this time I prepared a detailed report to send to Christine in the USA, accompanied by sketches of the house I intended to build, so that she would get some idea of what her domain would be when she rejoined me. I also informed Muana Cuca of what the future would bring in his life. I had expected that he would show some concern about having to work and share "his kitchen" with a *M'sisse* (wife), but his reaction was a total surprise to me. Deep creases appeared on his forehead (a sure sign that he was concentrating on some deep matter); then he looked up at me and said that he must go to the M'bua Mission. He would prepare easy meals that I could cook for myself while he was away, "about one week, maybe."

When I inquired why he had to go to the mission, the answer was, "I hear you say once that your *M'sisse* is Italian. The priests at M'bua are Italian and they taught their cook how to make Italian meals. I must go there (one week, no more) to learn how to cook so your *M'sisse* likes my food and don't send me away!"

When we started construction in earnest, the first action taken was to enclose a natural spring in a clean space, and prevent direct access from the outside. The water collected in a concrete tank, and from there the distribution piping originated. The tank was enclosed in a sturdy concrete ring with a locked iron door.

A brick-making operation was the next activity that got under way. The brick-makers found the correct type of clay that they needed and started to dig it out following their ancient way of removing the top soil in narrow strips, then digging out the clay layer underneath using short-handled hoes. The void left by removing the clay was filled afterward with the topsoil that they had piled by the side of the trench. No scars were left on the site, and only a slight depression, soon occupied by bushes and weeds, bore witness to the removal of the clay.

The clay was transported in wheelbarrows to a pit where four men blended it by kneading with their feet for hours, walking in the sticky mass in a trance-like, slow motion, rhythmic dance. (The wheelbarrows were my contribution to modernizing Africa, because the traditional way was to put the clay on top of short wooden boards and carry it balanced on their heads.)

Next, we cut logs of suitable timber in the forest. For this operation I had obtained a license from the authorities that allowed the company to cut just enough timber for our needs, and that stated the Latin names of the specific species we were allowed to cut. Since I had by then forgotten most of the Latin I had learned in school, and the Achirima workers had not ever heard of such a language, we compromised: we only cut the kinds that we needed!

After the logs had dried for a period of a few weeks, we shipped them to Mocubela where the company had a factory that produced wooden boxes. The boxes were used to export tea from the extensive plantations of Gurúe. This factory was equipped with modern machinery capable of handling any kind of lumber, and they turned the logs into boards and beams of the various sizes that we would need for construction of the new residences.

I had hired all the carpenters available in the surrounding villages. They constructed hundreds of wooden brick forms, then the already-blended clay was made into balls by hand and pressed into the molds. The filled molds were placed on top of long boards and carried by two men, one in front and the other at the back, to a wide flat area where the bricks were pushed out of the molds and left to dry for over a week.

The next stage was to build the kilns. By then the bricks had developed enough green strength to allow them to be handled with care and they were piled carefully, leaving open passageways between so that heated air could travel throughout the kiln and bake them. These passages were first filled with dry twigs. Then, the whole kiln was covered with a special coat of clay plastered by hand. After this outside cover had dried, the kiln was fired by setting alight the twigs that filled the inside air passages. A crew kept adding dry wood to the front opening of the kiln, day and night, for three days. Afterwards the kiln sat for nearly a week, cooling gradually to avoid thermal shock that would crack the bricks if they cooled too quickly. Finally, the outside covering of clay was removed, and the bricks were allowed to cool completely.

While the first kiln was cooling, the brick makers repeated the performance with the next one. In all, ten kilns were built, fired, and subsequently dismantled, to remove the bricks after they had cooled. These bricks, which required such careful and elaborate handling, would be used for the load-bearing walls.

All the partition walls on the inside of the buildings would be built with adobe bricks,[36] formed in molds that were larger than those used for the fired bricks. Once filled, the adobe molds were set on the ground on top of a bed of grass. They were covered with a blanket of grass held down with stones so that the wind would not carry it away. It took over a week for the adobe to dry sufficiently such that the bricks could be removed manually from the grass bed and piled for complete drying under a shed made of wood poles holding up a grass roof.

The art of making East African adobe supposedly originated in the south of the Arabian Peninsula, probably in the ancient kingdom of the Sabeans (from whence came the Queen of Saba, referred to in the Bible). This was a land that from time immemorial maintained commercial ties with Mozambique. Judging from ancient buildings that still exist on Mozambique Island, adobe bricks were in use before the Sixteenth Century.[37] This style of adobe does not use straw mixed into the wet-molded mass, as I have seen in the southwestern USA and heard of in southern California. I have been told that the straw reinforces the strength of the adobe, but I doubt whether it is really worth the trouble to add straw and suspect that the only thing it does for sure is provide convenient tunnels for termites to get into the buildings.

In South Africa and many other regions where it is available, cow dung is incorporated into the mixture. However in the area I am writing about, there were no cattle due to the presence of tsetse fly. (Tsetse flies transmit sleeping sickness, which is lethal to cattle.) Instead, we added some of the material from which termite nests are made. I was told that it is just as good as cow dung for making an "everlasting adobe."

While all these various preliminary operations were in progress, employing dozens of African workers and requiring efficient scheduling and logistics, the mines that constituted the main reason for our varied interests had to continue to operate. They required guidance and supplies of food, explosives, tools, and spare parts for the machinery used to produce the minerals we exported. I had constant and very competent assistance from the surveyor in supervising the construction operations, but the mining operations required that I spread myself thinner and thinner, until I was beginning to become translucent.

After the roof of corrugated iron sheets had been put on my house, I concluded that the next steps towards giving it the final touches could go on without my supervision. I told the president that I needed a vacation. Christine and Danny had been staying with her parents in the USA while I established a base in which they would be safe. Now I got on the road to join them, and at the end of my vacation I would bring them back to Napido Town, Gilé Post, County of Alto Molócuè, District of Zambezia, Mozambique.

Commercial flying in those days was more complicated than it is now, and it was a very different experience. The planes were slower and it took much longer to get to your destination. Their range was limited so we hopped up the west coast of Africa to reach Europe. On the plus side, because they flew at lower altitudes you could really see what the countries down below looked like. And the planes were a lot more comfortable then than they are now!

In order to join my family in Denver, Colorado, I began the journey with a day's drive to Quelimane. From there, I flew the next day to Lourenço Marques. Two days later, I flew to Lisbon, Portugal with stops in the Belgian Congo, Ghana, and Senegal. The following day I flew across the Atlantic to New York City. The final day of travel took me to Chicago and at last to Denver.

My stay in the United States was occupied by contacts with relatives and with friends from my days at the Colorado School of Mines. I visited the Denver Bureau of Mines and some mining installations. My preferred occupation was playing with little Danny, who was by then a toddler. He had a red wagon which he pulled with him everywhere, and he used to carry any rocks he found to Daddy for classification. The days went by so quickly that it soon was time to return to East Africa.

We flew first to New York and from there to Rome, where we visited with some of Christine's relatives. Then we flew on to East Africa via Khartoum in the Sudan and Johannesburg, South Africa. The trip back up to Zambezia was just a short hop to Quelimane where I had left my car. The next day, thanks to the new bridge over the Melela River, we reached Napido. Christine started to become acquainted with her new house and get used to relying on Muana Cuca who, to our great surprise, served us a complete Italian menu for our first meal.

My "new and improved" residence in Napido Town. Made of handmade bricks, and with inside walls formed from adobe blocks, it was surrounded by a wide veranda to keep the interior cooler. The "lawn" in front was an expanse of wild succulent plants that produced vibrant fuchsia flowers year-round. Photo by the author.

CHAPTER TWELVE

Munha Morros' Mines

After my return, I was in camp inspecting the foundations for the next house to be built in Napido Town when a man arrived on a noisy and dusty motorbike. He introduced himself as the owner of "a parcel of beryl claims that your president is interested in and that you are supposed to examine." I had already received instructions over the radio about this matter, and was ready to follow the visitor to his mining properties. Christine had been invited to spend a few days with the family of the *chefe de posto*, and she decided to take this opportunity to visit them while I was away.

I packed the necessary gear into the Beetle and followed the man over the Morrua Bridge and then across country, following bush trails trending roughly to the southwest. We reached his house just before darkness fell. He owned a coffee plantation, and also produced tobacco and sesame and owned large herds of cattle.

Among his native neighbors who lived in villages surrounding the plantation, he was known by the African name *Munha Morro*, which translates from the Lomwe dialect as *The One Who Farts Fire*. This name came from the fact that he had arrived in the area riding a smoking, bad-smelling, and noisy motorbike—a strange vehicle that the Lomwe had never seen before!

I spent the night in an enormous adobe building covered with a grass roof. Inside there were tables made of hand-hewn hardwood planks, some chairs, and a couple of huge sofas. There were mineral samples laying everywhere: on the hard earth floor, on the tables, on the sofas. Most of the specimens were quartz crystals. But there were also some nice pieces of aquamarine in matrix, and beryl crystals of all sizes. The room had a pervasive aroma, with expected overtones of cat and dog smells. But there was also a background scent of dried tobacco leaves and the acrid, irritating smell of cashew nuts burnt in their shells. Besides those, I could identify cooking smells—roasted meat and oven-baked sweet potatoes—and once in a while, the wind also brought whiffs from the corrals that seemed to be farther from the house.

The next three days were spent following the man on the motorbike along goat tracks and over flimsy bridges that he had built just strong enough to support himself and his bike. In his opinion, "a Volkswagen car does not weigh much more than a motorbike and, even if it falls through, we can pull it out with a dozen men." We talked about the area where the plantation was situated, about which I knew nothing. It was drained by the Nipiodi River and countless of its subsidiaries. From what I had observed while driving, the native rocks were metamorphic (originally sediments and volcanic rocks). Many hills, covered with quartz pieces, attested to the presence of pegmatites. I had expected that this area would, geologically speaking, be outside the Alto Ligonha Pegmatite District, but it was evident that I was dead wrong. In fact, I observed that its petrology was similar to that of the Alto Ligonha and that pegmatite bodies were widespread.

He owned mining claims spread over a very large area. All of them had been prospected by means of trenches exposing the pegmatite veins only to a shallow depth, but showing the mineralized zones well enough to give an idea of their value. It was evident that our itinerary had been planned with much care. Every evening we reached some village where the headman was expecting us and had built a grass-covered shed under which we spread our blankets for the night's rest. We were always served a good evening meal of *piri-piri* chicken, roasted manioc, and fresh fruits.[38]

When we returned to the plantation, I told him that three of his claims had the potential to develop into profitable mines.

"I am glad," he replied. "Are you going to evaluate the others as well? It would be useful for me to have a professional report. I might want to sell some of the others."

"Certainly," I said. "My report will mention every claim individually, identified with the numbers and names you gave me. I will write up the report and send you a copy before the end of this month."

"Good. I cannot pay you at the moment. But I'll find some way of settling your bill."

Some weeks later, back in Napido, I arrived home later than usual and bone-tired after a day of visiting various mines separated from each other by many miles of rough roads across the forest. Christine and Danny had already gone to bed. After a shower I sat down to a bowl of soup, intending to turn in and go to sleep as soon as I finished my meal. At that moment, Fernando gave me the news that the debt had been paid with a truckload of pregnant goats! As soon as

I finished my soup, Fernando handed me a letter that read, "As usual, the Planters' Cooperative is behind in their payments and, since I do not know when they are going to pay for last year's tobacco crop, I have decided to send you a small herd of goats in settlement of the account. They are all female and pregnant—except for the ram, naturally."

Fernando wanted to discuss the building of a corral for the animals and the hiring of a goatherd but I said, "The only thing that I want right now is a cup of coffee, and fast, before I fall asleep right here, at the table. Go make it, and we will talk goats tomorrow; *muhiua pama?*"[39]

The next morning before the family was up, I sat down for a relaxed breakfast on the wide verandah that ran around three-quarters of the house. A man approached, leading a powerfully-built black ram by a short rope. He introduced himself as a professional goatherd.

"A man from Nipiodi came yesterday. He has his truck full of *purri* (goats). He stop at *Muéne* Napido's village and he ask if he can unload his *purri* at the chief's corral, until you have finished building a corral of your own for your very beautiful animals. Because the *purri* were for you, but you no have no corral, the chief, he say yes, but he call me to take care of your animals which are all very beautiful.

"Animals like this cannot be mixed with the chief's *purris* that have many diseases. Therefore, I come here this morning, to catch you before you go to work, to say I know how to take good care of these *purris*. I know how to build a good, strong corral so that no *havarra* nor *Karramo*[40] can get in.

"I know what happened three nights ago, when your night watchmen that go around this camp during the night, had to hide in that hut where the machine-that-makes-light[41] is, and they had to lock themselves in until morning because a very big *Karramo* was walking up and down the streets of this camp, right in the middle of the streets, like he owns this place. When the *Karramo* walk around like that, you please excuse me for saying so, but you need to build a very, very strong corral, you need to lock all the doors, and you need to sleep with a loaded rifle under your bed.

"People think that *Karramo* is stupid, and it is true. He only uses his weight to kill. *Havarra* does not do things like that. He walk around this camp and he see and remember where everything is, and if there is anything that he can kill and eat, he study all the ways he can get to it and kill it and then get away without anybody seeing him.

"So, we have to build a corral for your *purris* with strong poles pushed deep into the ground that *Karramo* cannot overthrow with his weight. To keep *havarra* out is much more difficult because he is a cat and is very clever. But I know his tricks."

As he finished talking, Fernando came with coffee and freshly-made toast and placed the food on a small table near me. I started to butter a piece of toast, and at the same moment the goatherd freed the ram from the lead rope. The animal came straight to me, studied me at leisure, and then concentrated on smelling the toast and looking up at my face as if he were suggesting that the least I could do, would be to let him taste this new food. The gesture was so natural that I gave him the buttered toast, just as I would do to any human guest who had shown so much interest in tasting some dish unknown to him. The ram accepted the toast, chewed it very calmly and then sat down by my chair.

The goatherd and I discussed at length the location and construction details of a corral, where my goats could spend their nights free from the terror of roaming marauders. I gave the green light for the project, then got up to go to the office.

The goatherd, rope in hand, moved to tie-up the ram, but never got to it. The animal, without showing any signs of nervousness, simply moved to the other side of me, placing himself out of reach. As I started walking to the office, it took position close to my left thigh and stayed there until I opened the front door of the office building and went in. I signaled to the goatherd, who had followed us at a distance, to go away and leave it. Through the window, I observed its behavior. It watched the door of the office for a few minutes. Then it moved away towards the edge of the forest that enclosed the camp, and started to graze.

After reading a lot of reports that were on my desk, I got up to go visit the minerals treatment plant which was some distance down the main street of the camp. As I stepped out, the ram approached, took up his position on my left flank, and walked with me to the entrance of the treatment plant. He made no attempt to go into that noisy place, but instead found some shade and sat there quietly.

Everywhere I went, from that day on, the ram took this position. Danny sometimes accompanied me on my rounds to the minerals-sorting plant and to various other facilities located on the campus. When he did, he would hold onto my right hand, while the ram stayed in position by my left thigh—as long as it was during his "working hours." In late afternoons, he led his harem to drink in the river, then walked back to the corral at the head of the herd. He would wait for all of them to go through the main gate of the corral, which had been built a good distance from the back of my house, and watch from the inside until the goatherd had secured the heavy door of the enclosure.

It did not take long for the personnel to give the ram a nickname: he was christened "The Bodyguard."

CHAPTER THIRTEEN

A Change in the Weather[42]

Up until the end of 1959, our company enjoyed an excellent relationship with members of the various African tribes who worked for us at the mines and in a variety of other jobs that we offered. Naturally from time to time there were disagreements, misunderstandings, and differences of opinion, and these were handled according to a policy I had established. The men in charge of African employees had to follow the following procedures strictly, whenever there was a conflict.

If an incident occurred between African employees belonging to the same tribe, the overseer in charge would call in a group leader of that same tribe. He would ask the leader to talk with both parties involved and try to re-establish peace between them. If the group leader did not succeed in solving the problem, the two parties would be sent to their tribal chief to resolve their differences.

If a conflict happened between members of different tribes, every reasonable precaution would be taken to avoid an outbreak of tribal warfare—which could start as a result of even minor arguments. The mine superintendent would try to find a solution that in no way made one of the parties lose face. If this attempt failed, the case would immediately be reported to the local Portuguese authorities, which for ninety percent of our mines meant the *chefe de posto* of Gilé. Until the *chefe de posto* arrived or sent a representative, the two parties would be transferred to working areas far from where the conflict had occurred, in order to avoid the formation of partisan groups supporting either side.

In rare situations where disagreement took place between a European and an African, the case had to be reported to me immediately. I would study it and find a solution that would not cause loss of face for either party, or even the slightest trace of anything that might be construed as racism. These situations, which rarely occurred in Mozambique, usually resulted in both parties being transferred to different places.

I had discussed my policy and procedures with the African chiefs when we had first started hiring local workers. Every one of the chiefs had agreed with me that the regulations were fair and that they provided adequate means of preventing simple, everyday problems from developing into serious conflicts. The chiefs knew that the Government of Mozambique took very seriously the existence of a peaceful status quo among the indigenous tribes, and that it was enforced very strictly. The Portuguese authorities delegated most of the responsibility for maintaining peaceful relations among the African populations, to the chiefs.

Most of the mine superintendents we employed had years of experience dealing with tribal natives. Nevertheless, I constantly urged them not to forget that each of our good-natured, ever-laughing, -dancing, and -singing employees still remembered every detail of ancient, bitter, and merciless wars among their ancestors. The memory of ancient conflicts among different tribes was maintained through stories told to the children around the village fires every evening, and re-enacted in their ritual dances. Distrust and dislike among adjacent tribal groups was thus kept very much alive and played a very important role in their modern relations with each other.

If an outsider wishes to understand the profound distrust that exists between neighboring African tribes, he must learn to listen and interpret the meaning of legends that refer in symbolic, child-like stories and rituals, to real happenings of long ago. These legends, which deal mostly with wars, catastrophes, invasions and calamities, are the living archives of each tribe's history. It is also fundamental to take into consideration that the African understanding of terms and concepts including nationality, citizenship, and democracy, do not coincide with European definitions.

The history of African "nations" during the time for which we have records, shows that they existed only for limited periods. A tyrant would subjugate the tribes of a given area, organize a mighty army, and rule over a large empire only as long as he and his family could destroy their rivals. Eventually they would be destroyed themselves, and the "empire" would shatter and divide itself into small tribal groups again. The only consistently human organization was always the tribe.

Many writers interested in African affairs have offered their judgments on the roles played by the various colonial powers in the development of the African peoples. One writer arrived at the conclusion that, "the heritage of law and order left by the White Man was the most precious gift." True enough, I would agree— as long as the colonial powers were present to enforce their style of "law and order." However, they did this by ignoring the fact that they were destroying the powers that had been vested in the traditional African chiefs and used to enforce their centuries-old system of "law and order." And now look at what has happened, since the departure of the colonial system!

In the general area around our company's mines, our structured approach worked quite well at first. We had policies in place to deal with any serious outbreaks of tribal disputes, and the policies were understood by the Africans and their tribal leaders and enforced by me and the company. Everyone understood that I had the backing of the government authorities should there be a need to appeal to them for help. I seldom had to go and visit with the African chiefs to refresh their memories about the need for action when, for example, members of their tribe had committed heinous sins such as taking liberties with women of another tribe or cutting a tree without first investigating which village owned the tree and asking permission to cut it. We had all lived in peace and had enjoyed friendly relations based on mutual respect, since the time when our company had started prospecting for mineral deposits and had subsequently opened the mines.

But suddenly at the end of 1959, a very sudden and marked change occurred in the status quo. The first sign that something was not as it should be, was a sharp increase in absenteeism among the workers at most of the mines. This was accompanied by their loss of focus on safety and consequentially, a sudden increase in accidents caused by laziness and inattention. At some locations, the pilfering of food and small tools from the warehouses started to become common. All of the mine superintendents complained that in a rather short period of time, exemplary workers who had always been reliable, responsible, and amiable people had become irresponsible and absent-minded fools, who required constant pushing to complete their tasks.

In response, I mounted a counter-offensive during which I held talks with the mine superintendents and the African group leaders of our work force. I explained that without the responsible performance of everyone's jobs, the mines could not make the money necessary to pay their salaries. The mines would have to be closed, bringing unemployment for the men and suffering for their families.

My efforts were met with little success, and a few weeks later I started the next phase of my diplomatic endeavors. I arranged visits of ceremony with the chiefs, held in the presence of their councils of elders. These meetings were convened at prearranged dates and took place in the special huts reserved for the discussion of matters that affect tribal power. All of the complex steps of African protocol and ceremony were staged and followed meticulously.

Previously, I had always enjoyed excellent relations with the chiefs, and I tried to be as patient as possible in presenting my arguments. I used lengthy and detailed examples to help the tribal leaders realize that: the clinics we maintained at every mine; the schools where their people received free education, free books, and other services; and the stores where we sold them articles at cost, would all have to be discontinued if the mines stopped working at a profit. I made it very clear that, if their subjects did not come back to work and the mines were forced to import outside laborers, the locals would lose access to the free facilities (such as the schools and clinics) that we maintained for them and their families, as well as for everyone else in the surrounding village populations. I also added that in the event we were forced to close down the mines, their people would be seriously affected economically. We regularly bought all their excess corn and other farm production, and had always helped them transport their cotton to market. Without the use of our trucks, they would be unable to get their main cash crop to market. I always ended by asking the chiefs to encourage the men to become more responsible, in the interest of their own families, even if they did not care for the company's economic success.

The chiefs and their councils received me with courtesy, respect and, in most villages, with friendliness. Some of the chiefs agreed with my points, and they made half-hearted promises to the effect that they would "talk to the men." Others seemed embarrassed; they did not have any arguments to present, and I had the impression that they were reluctantly obeying orders from somebody else. A few chiefs received my visit with veiled hostility, while politely avoiding any promises of counseling their subjects about anything. In previous years, the chiefs' honest concern for the welfare of their subjects had always been evident. Unfortunately, it seemed that this concern had suddenly evaporated into shallow pretense, which reminded me of politicians during election times. I was strongly disillusioned and alarmed about the deterioration of working conditions in our mines. But I was saddened even more by the way this society, which had been exemplary in its respect for human values, had become cynical and corrupt in such a short time.

While the climate of unrest continued to develop, and I carried out a diplomatic campaign to resolve it, there were some instances in which humorous situations developed. One of these was at the Namivo Mine, which was probably the richest beryl deposit ever found in the world. The mine employed about 100 men, because it contained gem grade aquamarine that had to be hand-sorted to separate the semi-precious material from the commercial grade ore.

At the Namivo Mine, the men had continued to report to work as before. But they would leave the mine pit to go to the toilets and stay away for hours before returning, only to lounge about talking in little groups and not doing their usual work. Zacharias, the mine superintendent, had up until then been a very popular person amongst the workers. He was even the coach and goalkeeper of their soccer team. He reasoned with the workers and went to talk with Chief Namivo, but got nowhere. Even after talking to the workers myself and initiating a program of cash bonuses to keep them interested in their tasks, I found that the results were not encouraging. I kept on visiting the mine more often than before. One day I arrived, and the first thing I asked the superintendent was the usual, "How is the problem? Any improvement?"

Zacharias answered with an encouraging smile. "Yes, it is solved. Come and take a look."

He led me to the edge of the pit, and I looked down into the deep hole. There I saw a large number of workers in small groups, each group busily performing its specific task. Near each group, I noticed a brightly painted bamboo stick driven into the ground. What immediately struck me was the fact that the mine had recaptured its normal aspect of a busy and well-organized enterprise. I turned to Zacharias and said, "Congratulations! How did you manage to get them back to work? And what are those painted sticks for?"

"I assembled the men and told them that I was getting so tired of going around enticing them to get back to work and to do this and do that, without any success. I said that I had come to understand how tired they must be of listening to me harassing them all the time. I explained that I was prepared to shut up and leave them in peace, if they agreed to play a game. Each team that performed a special task in the mine would have its own stick painted with any color that they liked, different from the colors used by other teams.

"These sticks would be pushed into the ground near the place where they worked. If any member of a group wanted to leave work and go some place, as long as he took with him the stick of their team I would not upbraid, interfere with, nor ask where he was going, or how long he would be away from work. But, *if I caught anybody loafing without the stick of his team,* he would have to listen to me.

"They liked the idea of the game and the fun of shutting me off. So, they chose their favorite colors and cut their sticks. I gave them paint to cover the sticks, and soon the game started. They are all having great fun, watching me to see if I can keep my big mouth shut."

"It seems to be working," I said. "But I don't get the point. If a fellow can take his group's stick to go loafing about without having you scold him, why don't the others do the same?" I asked.

"Because," Zacharias answered, "they all want to enjoy the privilege of strutting leisurely past me with the stick under their arms and forcing me to keep my mouth shut. But no one else can do it until the stick is brought back. So, the other members of the group put pressure on the fellow to hurry back. That's the whole secret of the scheme!"

CHAPTER FOURTEEN

The Storm

During 1960, things went from bad to worse. I continued to visit with the chiefs and tried patiently to make them understand: the absenteeism and irresponsibility that had become widespread among their subjects would force me to start recruiting personnel from other tribes, and their people would lose access to the facilities that they enjoyed. However, I achieved nothing in practical terms. It seemed that either the chiefs did not bother to talk sense to their subjects, or that there was a concerted action underway in which the chiefs were also engaged.

Eventually the company had to go recruiting far to the west and to the south, in the areas of the *postos* of Mulevala and Mocubela. The tribesmen from these areas had never worked in mines, and they had to be put through a lengthy training period. The additional training increased considerably the already high cost of labor. Also, special camps had to be built for the new arrivals, because if we put them together with (or even near) the locals, then fights would start as soon as everyone returned to camp after work.

I had warned the local chiefs repeatedly that if their people did not come to work in our mines, then we would not be able to keep the schools open (which we maintained at our cost for the use of their children). Nor would we be able to keep the clinics open (which provided treatment of simple ailments for all the nearby population, whether family members worked in the mines or not). Nor would the stores remain open (where we sold food and supplies at cost). Now we were gradually forced to close down one facility after another, because our labor costs had shot up, while at the same time the efficiency of the workers had gone down to near-zero, and the theft of food, tools, and various supplies was constantly increasing. The same chiefs I had cautioned began blaming me for the negative impact on their subjects.

During the first years of our operations we had been the only company in a huge area, and we built the roads and bridges that opened access to the area. By this time, there were many other companies and individuals doing business in the area, with whom we maintained cordial relations. From conversations with these neighbors, I learned that the attitude of passive resistance towards employers was widespread. Many of the managers of the other companies were convinced that this was a concerted policy directed from outside Mozambique, and designed to destroy the good racial relations that had existed for a long time in the country. Mutual respect between whites and blacks, which had been the norm in this country, made the leaders of the newly independent countries such as Zambia and Tanzania green with envy.

Some of our neighbors pointed out similarities with the Mau-Mau movement that had wrecked the Kenyan economy. Others thought the conditions were a natural result either of incompetent mismanagement by the Lisbon authorities or of the just aspirations for self-determination on the part of the Mozambicans. Everyone agreed that it was time for Portugal to accept that its policies had failed and let the locals (of all colors) play a more active role in the government of the country.

In July of 1960, a most disturbing and tragic incident occurred in northern Mozambique, in a town near the Tanzanian border. A large mob, incited to violence by two well-known troublemakers from Tanzania, congregated in front of the administration building in Mueda. They demanded the release of two family members of the Tanzanian leaders. The District Administrator informed the crowd that the people in question had only been summoned as witnesses in a civil case and that they had made their depositions and gone home.

The two activists, clearly seeking an excuse to get the mob into a fighting mood, then demanded that the government force businessmen to pay higher prices for the crops that they bought from the locals. Furthermore, they demanded that salaries paid to workers in the area be raised. The District Administrator explained that he had no control over such matters and suggested that, since the Governor of the district was due to visit the area on a routine visit, they should present their demands to him.

The Governor arrived three days later, but the army escort that was supposed to accompany him did not show up. Instead, he was met by an excited crowd of about 5,000 Maconde tribesmen who surrounded him, knocked him down, and trod on him. This caused the local African policemen to open fire on the mob, in order to extricate the Governor and get him into the building. Just after the rioters calmed down and as the participants were beginning to think that they had over-reacted, the Governor's army escort appeared. Without consulting the Governor, they opened fire on the crowd causing heavy casualties.

Subversive propaganda about the Mueda incident was broadcast from Tanzania and reached the area of our concession, located more than 500 kilometers from the border. The one visible effect caused by the news was that the natives started to go around armed with spears, machetes, and even bows and arrows. This caused me to visit the chiefs once again. I wanted to learn the reason why people who never before had shown any signs of belligerency, were now going around armed. They avoided contact with us and hid in the bush when they saw our cars going past them.

I was told by some that I must be mistaken, because they had not seen anybody going around armed except for groups that were formed, once in a while, to go hunting for baboons to eat. Others said that they had heard the Portuguese were attacking and killing African people in Angola, and they expected the same would soon start happening in Mozambique. When I asked where this news came from, nobody would admit that they owned a "saucepan" radio or that they were listening to propaganda broadcast from Tanzania. Nor would they listen when I patiently explained that what actually had happened in Angola was exactly the other way around. Members of an African movement led by Holden Roberto[43] had, for no apparent reason, massacred hundreds of unarmed Portuguese farmers.

After my visits to the chiefs, I called on the *chefe de posto* of Gilé and told him that what I had heard from the chiefs meant only one thing: somebody, or some organized group, was intimidating the locals with threats and spreading false rumors. The intention was apparently to create unrest amongst the tribes and eventually turn them against the Portuguese. I suggested that he inform his superiors of the situation so that the authorities could counter all this with factual information. The *chefe de posto* told me that he had informed his superiors all along of what was happening, but had not received any acknowledgement or any instructions on how to proceed.

The situation continued to deteriorate slowly but surely, and the next development occurred the following year. A group of nurses led by a doctor arrived at Napido Camp, traveling in a caravan of new American cars and a mobile clinic. I had been informed that this was a program sponsored by the World Health Organization. The goal was to vaccinate the African populations in order to eradicate a venereal disease that was prevalent in the area. In accordance with the request from the authorities, I had assembled all our workers in an empty warehouse where the medical personnel gave every man one injection.

The cars in which the medical personnel traveled were driven by Africans who, it was rumored some time later, were members of FRELIMO. As our men left after their vaccinations, the drivers told each person that the injection they had just received was a powerful *mitombo* (witchcraft medicine) produced by the most famous witchdoctor of Tanzania. The *mitombo* would make them immune to the White Man's bullets. From then on, the men need not be afraid to attack the police or the armed forces, whose bullets had been made soft by the *mitombo* and would not kill them.

The nurse in charge of our clinic at Napido was a serious and dedicated African man, of the Maganja tribe. I remember him asking me after the medial caravan left if I had heard a broadcast from Tanzania. The announcer said that the tribes in our general area had been made immune to death by White Man's bullets. Furthermore, the broadcast claimed that the proof of this was that the Fascist Government of Mozambique had ordered the execution of all African men of military age, but that nobody had died during the executions.

I said, "I don't listen to that rubbish. You know that the government does not do stupid things like that, neither here nor anywhere else. Why do you listen to it?"

"I don't usually listen, but I was trying to tune into a program of African music when I heard somebody talking in the language of this area with a funny accent. I was curious to hear what these stupid Lomwe had to say."

By 1964, after many attempts to create a united political party in Mozambique had ended in bitter tribal arguments and disagreements, an American citizen of Mozambican origin had become the leader of FRELIMO. He ordering an attack on a small settlement named Chai, located south of the Mozambique-Tanzania border. The local police put up a fight, but they were wiped out by the well-armed and well-trained attackers. Chai was completely destroyed, and all the population was massacred.

A few months later, one of our trucks was on the road to the Port of Pebane carrying a load of beryl for export to the USA. On a very isolated stretch of road, the African driver saw what looked like a fence built across the road from bamboo and tree branches. The driver interpreted the obstacle as an ambush and had the presence of mind to put on speed, crash through it, and keep going. When he arrived at Pebane, he went straight to the authorities. He reported the incident and offered to lead the police to the place. His offer was accepted, an armed police patrol was organized, and they returned to the location indicated by the driver without any opposition. They found that the fence had been removed hastily, but enough signs had been left behind to back the driver's story. The police patrol included an experienced tracker, who soon found the spoor of a group of five or six men moving quickly away from the site. After awhile they had split up and moved away in various directions. As darkness approached, the police patrol had to give up the search.

I reported the incident to our headquarters and suggested that we request military escorts for our trucks and travel in organized convoys. I also recommended including trucks from our neighbors at the tantalite mine across the river. They had reported that, on more than one occasion, their trucks had been stoned by groups of African children who subsequently disappeared into the forest.

Soon after these incidents, the president called me back to company headquarters in Quelimane. He briefed me on the outcome of various meetings at which the authorities had promised him they would study the situation; however, they had not contacted him again. We considered the options and finally reached a decision to start closing down the mines. I would begin immediately by starting to close down the mines with the highest operating costs. I estimated the time it would take to clean up the areas around the mines, make the pits safe, and remove the equipment. The staff at headquarters would find new jobs for the skilled personnel. The African laborers released from mines as they ceased operations would be transferred to those mines that were still running. The laborers that could not be placed would be paid a monetary compensation for the time still left on their contracts and would be transported back to their home villages. All recruiting of new laborers would stop forthwith.

Of course, the closures would impact the larger mines where we had installed facilities for the use of the local workers and their families (the schools, clinics, and stores). The operational costs of these facilities came to a considerable expense. After my return to the field, I sent word to the chiefs that the schools would be closed at the end of the present semester. I advised them to warn parents that they should register their children at the government schools instead. I also told them that the clinics would stay open only as long as the existing stock of medicines lasted. The same criterion would apply to the stores: they would stay open until their stocks ran out.

When I had brought to the attention of these same chiefs their subjects' sudden and inexplicable laziness and irresponsible behavior, they had been unconcerned. Now, they came and threatened me with complaints to the authorities if I closed down the facilities their people utilized. I replied that I had warned them more than once this would happen, but they had not paid any attention. Now, they could go to the authorities if they wished!

I grew concerned though, and I feared that shutting the mines would result in acts of violence against me, and possibly against my family. Christine and Daniel had been living with me at Napido since the house had been built, but six months after the decision was made to close the mines I concluded that they must return to Lourenço Marques. I drove them to say good-bye to our many friends in the government offices and at the other mining and farming enterprises in the large area around Napido. Then I took them to Mozambique Island, where they boarded a ship bound for Lourenço Marques. Once there, they would open up our house near the city and await my return.

Despite my concern, there were no attempts to attack me personally. I was always treated with respect and, in many places, with signs of friendliness. The Africans I had worked with more regularly seemed to be conveying with their manners that which they were afraid to say in words: "We are being forced to destroy the evidence that the White Man has done good things for us. We have to destroy the economy of this country; we have to force the commercial and industrial organizations to shut down; but we do not hold you personally responsible for anything."

It took more than a year to wind down all the operations. Every skilled employee was offered an alternate job; every mine was reclaimed and excavations were filled in; buildings were left clean and locked; and the keys were handed over to the *chefe de posto*. All equipment that became idle was sold or transported to Pebane for storage. I presided over the operations with a very heavy heart. I started to have insomnia, I lost my appetite, and I had to push myself to perform even the most routine tasks.

I had accepted the challenge to enter a wild, unknown, and remote area, to study its geology, and to find and develop its mineral deposits. In order to accomplish that task we had opened and operated a school where local men and outsiders learned the ancient art of prospecting for minerals. We had built roads and bridges, and mines had been opened and worked using state-of-the-art equipment. We had employed local men, built buildings to house them and schools where their children were taught to read and write. We had established clinics for the general population and stores where they bought needed goods at cost. In large part due to the efforts of our group, Mozambique had become the world's leading producer of beryl, and the second-largest producer of tantalite.

I was deeply saddened. I was presiding over the erasure of material proof that the challenge I had accepted, had been realized. Once I was sure that remaining personnel could finish the task, I asked to be released of my duties.

My last acts were three important visits. First, I traveled the 150 kilometers north, to personally thank the missionaries of the M'bua Mission for their kindness to all our personnel. On the way back I stopped at the administrative post in Gilé and paid my respects to the *chefe de posto*. He had become a disheartened, disillusioned man. The following day, I traveled west to Novanana and said goodbye to the old chief. It was very difficult to hold his hands and look into his wrinkled face for the last time. I still remember the sadness registered there.

I heard, years later, that he and most of the leaders of the Achirima people were hanged by the guerrillas.

CHAPTER FIFTEEN

A New Life

It had taken me six months after my family's departure to get the situation under control and leave the area. Once I was back in Lourenço Marques, I began to look for partners with the necessary capital to reopen an abandoned copper mine, named the Edmundian Mine. I had discovered the mine back in 1952 when I studied the geology of the Zambuzi Valley, in the Manica District of Mozambique.[44] This District was situated near the border with Southern Rhodesia (now called Zimbabwe), in an area where the guerrillas did not dare operate. In those days, Rhodesia was under the Ian Smith regime and had a very efficient anti-guerrilla military force.

I found a group of businessmen, residents of South Africa and Rhodesia, who were interested in investing the necessary funds. I registered the mine with the Department of Mines, and moved the family to the nearest urban center: the historic town of Macequece (also known as Manica). Then I started the long and dangerous task of making old tunnels safe, and dewatering the deep underground mine that had closed down and filled with water after the First World War. It took 365 days of pumping, twenty-four hours per day, to reach the bottom of the main shaft, which was being filled with water by all the other tunnels. We reconditioned all the underground passageways and installed the equipment necessary to mine the ore, transport it to the surface, crush and concentrate it, and then pack it for export to Japan.

We enrolled Danny in the local grade school when we first arrived. He was in a classroom with over thirty children, who were mostly from the African villages surrounding Macequece. Danny could already read a little and spoke both Portuguese and English fluently; but he did not know Chimanica, the African language spoken by the other kids. Mozambique, like all African countries, has many languages and dialects. It was impossible to print schoolbooks and train teachers in every language. The solution was to have the African children learn first the official language in which the books were printed: Portuguese. This method put the African children back one or two years, but it also served to introduce them to the culture of the colonizing country and put them in contact with an outside world that they otherwise would not have known.

While his classmates worked on learning Portuguese, Danny became bored and uninterested. Christine visited the teacher, who suggested we withdraw him and put him in a mission school run by the Franciscan Friars. There he could follow a more advanced curriculum and be among schoolmates from his own environment.

During the years we worked the copper mine, guerrilla warfare gradually but steadily spread down from northern Mozambique to the center. Outrages were practiced on farmers and their families on both sides of the border. It became unsafe to travel. I had already seen similar occurrences before, and I had been in similar conditions. I could see that the military was continuing their attempt to fight African guerrillas with worn-out and unsuccessful European tactics. Another thing was becoming quite obvious. Back in Portugal, the fight for colonies they knew very little about was not popular with the population. And this was the case regardless how well a somber situation was gilded by propaganda produced by the big shots of the Salazar dictatorship.

My partners and I decided that before things got even worse, we would sell the mine. After the sale, Christine, Danny and I reopened our house near Lourenço Marques and spent a couple of months restoring and painting it, and making it habitable and comfortable again. Dan began attending the same high school that I attended when I first arrived in Mozambique.

I visited my colleagues at the Geological Survey of Mozambique to inquire whether there was any vacancy for which I might apply. I also wanted to pay my respects to the new director, who had been appointed recently. I had met him once before, but only briefly. I was received with much cordiality and was informed that the Government intended to create a department to promote the development of new mines. The director said that he would like to recommend me to lead that department, and he wondered if I would be interested.

"Yes, I would be interested to study your offer in detail," I answered.

He picked up the phone, asked the assistant director to come in, and introduced me to the man with whom I would work for the next few years. We eventually became good friends and developed a smooth working team in the new department. The department in turn contributed to the development of a large number of new mines.

I still recall the evening when I first told Christine and Dan that I had been offered this position. I said that I was thinking of accepting, and Christine was elated.

"I think that the job will suit you. And I am looking forward to living once again amongst people who come home from work every evening—people who dine out with friends once in a while or go out to enjoy a concert or some other 'civilized' function!"

The new department we started at the Geological Survey developed very well and, in a short time, became a valuable source of support for the mining industry. The expertise we provided was especially helpful during the crucial period between the discovery of a mineral deposit and a mine's first production of concentrates or ores.

Mozambique is extremely rich in certain rare minerals and specimens such as tantalite, columbite and beryl (to name a few), as well as in gems of unusual beauty. Extracting and preparing them for market requires highly specialized knowledge that the average prospector does not usually possess. Therefore, we concentrated on putting that specialized marketing know-how within reach of the prospectors. The increase in the quality and value of the country's mineral exports was notable.

Unfortunately, once again political and social unrest began to interfere with our assistance programs. Development of mines in the northern part of the territory was heavily impacted by the unsuccessful war being waged by the Portuguese Army against the guerrillas. Then on April 25, 1974, a group of Marxist army officers staged a coup in Lisbon and took over the government of Portugal. At that time, I was conducting a course for prospectors at Muiane. This mine is a famous one and the source of many of the most beautiful specimens of tourmaline crystals existing in museums and private collections. In the evening, we were enjoying pre-dinner drinks at the home of the mine manager and trying to hear news of the outside world through a short-wave radio. Through the thick static, we barely made out the first news of the coup in Portugal, followed by communist slogans and songs.

The next day, no students showed up for the lecture I was scheduled to give them. The mine manager reported that most of the mines had had to close because no employees reported for work. I met one of my students in the street and asked him why he had not come to my lecture.

"Don't you know there was a revolution in Portugal? The communists took over, and we don't have to work any more! The new government will give us independence and will feed and take care of us now!"

I couldn't help but recall that up until then, no one had admitted to owning a "saucepan radio," or even to knowing what one was!

A period of complete chaos followed, during which I tried to keep the Department operational. However, I was constantly losing personnel, and eventually I had to close down the laboratories for lack of supplies and operators.

In 1975, Danny finished high school. The University of Lourenço Marques, where I lectured on mining subjects, was suffering the same difficulties as my department. In order for Dan to get an opportunity to enter a decent college, we had to send him to the USA. Because the anti-American propaganda was increasing daily, we decided that both Christine and Dan should return to the States immediately; the climate was becoming too dangerous for American citizens. I applied for permission to send them enough money each month for their upkeep. However, I was allowed to send only a single lump sum of $700. I made up my mind then: I would stay only long enough to sell our house and retire. Then I would leave the country to join my family.

As it turned out, I was not able to sell the house. My retirement pension was denied on the grounds that I did not have the minimum number of years of service. And the department collapsed when the last of our technical and scientific personnel left.

I packed my mineral collection, a few paintings and books, and a few African carvings, and barely managed to get them into the last American cargo ship that called at the Port of Lourenço Marques. In order to make sure that our meager possessions were not stolen before they got onto the ship, I stayed with the container until it was loaded aboard. I stood on my feet in the hot sun from 6:00 a.m. until sunset, without anything to drink or to eat. The only relief available was leaning against the small container's shady side.

After all my efforts to save our hard-won assets had failed, I managed as soon as I could to get a seat on a flight to South Africa. I put my documents in a briefcase, closed the house with all the furniture inside, drained the car's gas tank, and closed the garage door. Then I took a taxi to the airport and got into one long queue. There I stood, once again, for several hours in the broiling sun. At the emigration desk, the official questioned me with rough manners.

"Where are you going?"

"To Johannesburg, South Africa," I answered, putting on my most stupid air, "to get this wisdom tooth removed." I pointed to my cheek. "It is driving me insane, and at the hospital here I'll have to wait five weeks before they will extract it. I'll be back at the end of the week."

"How much money are you taking with you?" he asked with the same threatening attitude.

"Ten thousand Escudos," I said.

"Let me see it, and don't lie. I can search you and arrest you if I find more."

I knew this was the limit allowed and had asked my bank for a traveler's check, which I showed him.

"All right. Be sure to return in a week's time. Next!"

I had previously bought and paid for a ticket from Johannesburg to Denver, Colorado. I stopped in Lisbon long enough to request a review before a Medical Board, for the purpose of requesting retirement. Grounds for my request were spinal injuries caused by driving four-wheel-drive vehicles through bush tracks in my geological work, during many years. I had attached a résumé which listed my geological investigations and the estimated mileage traveled (which came to an impressive figure!). The doctors were overwhelmed with thousands such requests. My résumé convinced them: they granted me my retirement, and allowed a small pension. In May of 1975, I arrived in Denver, Colorado with $10 in my pocket. I was fifty-five years old and ready to start looking for a new "American Challenge."

Epilogue

In the introduction to *An African Career*, I wrote:

> Gusts of confused, ill-informed, and naïve 'Winds of Change'—originally 'made in America,' but appropriated and distorted by smart-asses trained in Russia—have destroyed many wonderful things that Africa had. Recently, the continent has been ravaged by a generalized holocaust. It has become a nightmare. Senseless wars, fought for no other reason than the greed of leaders, have brought famine, genocide and carelessly abandoned minefields. But the people—like the grass after a wild fire—will always re-emerge with strength and vibrancy, to live like Africans and to be Africans.

Sooner than I would ever have thought possible, I had the opportunity to personally verify how true my conclusion was.

In 2002, I was invited to teach summer courses in mineralogy and gemology at the most remote of the campuses of the Catholic University of Mozambique. This facility is located in a town named Cuamba, which is 150 kilometers southwest of the southern tip of Lake Malawi.[45] Cuamba is on the railway that connects the Port of Nacala in northern Mozambique, to the Malawi city of Zomba. The area has been inhabited since pre-colonial days by the Ajawa, Nyanja, and Iao tribes, who lived well and peacefully from the profits made growing cotton, tobacco, and sesame (used to make a fine vegetable oil). Unfortunately, the Civil War that followed Mozambique's independence forced many of these people to leave and take refuge in Malawi. Some observers estimated that over two million people crossed the border in order to escape the indiscriminate massacres of the native peoples which were carried out by both sides of the conflict.

At the time of my visit, refugees had begun to return and were starting to settle down in new lands offered to them by the government of Mozambique. The campus in Cuamba had been given the special mission of providing technical and scientific support to the newly-returned expatriates. In programs that continue at this writing, the people are being taught how to grow cash crops, in addition to the traditional subsistence crops of corn, manioc, sweet potatoes, and beans. In the process of preparing their new fields for cultivation, the returnees were encountering gems such as aquamarine, tourmaline, garnet, and even the occasional ruby, at or near the surface. These discoveries soon attracted the attention of Mafia agents, who are present all over Tanzania and other neighboring territories, and who have control over the traffic in gems. The peasants were ignorant of the value of their finds and were selling their gemstones at ridiculously low prices.

To counteract this trend, the Catholic University decided to offer summer courses to anyone with enough education to follow the basic principles of mineral identification and practical gemology. I was invited to teach the first of these courses, and I accepted the challenge to go once more into a part of Mozambique that is rarely visited by outsiders. The area holds special appeal for me because I grew up there. In 1935, my parents had moved the family to Nampula[46] which is now on the same railway line as Cuamba. In Nampula, I had met a pioneer prospector who gave me a few samples of mica and my first lecture on minerals.

I began my journey in Algarve, the southernmost Province of Portugal, and traveled by car from my home in a tiny village to the airport in Faro. I flew north to Lisbon, then northwards again to Paris; from Paris, I flew south to Johannesburg; and from there east to Maputo, the capital city of Mozambique. The following day, I flew north to Beira where I stayed three days and participated in meetings with the president of the Catholic University.

From Beira I flew to Nampula, where I was supposed to catch the train to Cuamba. However, when I arrived in Nampula I was informed that unless there were VIP passengers, the first class coach would not be added to the train. Furthermore I was told, "You cannot buy a ticket to travel in third class because, in spite of the fact that they sell tickets for one and one half the number of seats in each third class coach, the tickets are usually sold out weeks ahead. Second class is exactly the same as third class, but costs much more."

I was trying to figure out the best way to get myself promoted to VIP status, when my host intervened. I had been graciously received in the home of Professor Frenk Smits, and he provided the solution when he informed me, "A truck from the Cuamba Campus came down this evening to take back some mechanical parts needed up there, and it will be returning tomorrow. You have a seat reserved right next to the driver. The truck will stop in front of this house at four o'clock in the morning, and you must be ready to jump in with your bag. You'd better get a good rest, because it will be a tiring trip!"

I remember thinking, "How European!" (Doctor Smits is Dutch.) "A simple trip to Cuamba that back in the 1970s had taken two and a half to three hours, now requires that one get to bed early to be rested for the ordeal!"

Four o'clock the next morning found me plus my bag in front of the house, dressed for the "great ordeal," sprayed with mosquito repellent, bush hat on my head, camera around my neck, and prepared to wait at least an hour for my transportation. Five minutes later, a truck materialized out of the darkness and slid to a stop in front of me. Some dark forms jumped out of the back, grabbed my bag, and threw it into the back where I could make out sundry boxes and drums, and human forms occupying the spaces in between. I stepped to the open front door with the intention of sitting near the driver as I had been told, but found three passengers already seated, occupying that space. There was a concerted movement of hands, and I felt myself lifted up, passed along, and seated smoothly and tightly near the driver!

For lack of anything appropriate to say, I looked towards the driver and said, "Good morning, everybody!"

In answer to which, I heard a refrain of many voices answering, "Good morning, sir."

The driver turned his head to the space behind him and asked, "Everybody ready? Then, let's go!"

At that moment my eyes had fully adjusted to the gloom, and I saw that behind the driver was a bench running the whole width of the truck, filled with two nuns and at least four ladies carrying small babies. We took off, and even before we were out of town the driver had to circle around huge holes in the street to avoid ponds of water with the characteristic smell of sewage. He crossed through some that he could not possibly avoid. I began to think seriously that Professor Smits' prophecy about a tiring trip might be accurate! The best description of the road I can offer is that it looked like it had been subjected to a barrage of heavy artillery.

I will leave the rest to the reader's imagination and will only contribute this much: it took ten hours to reach Cuamba. In the once-thriving small towns along the way, there was only one place where you could buy a warm, dust-covered bottle of Coca-Cola®. Nowhere was a bathroom to be found, but the driver stopped a few times in places where there were trees near the road to announce, "Ladies can go to the right, men to the left. Watch out for snakes, and don't take too long, please!"

We also stopped various times, in order to assist other vehicles that had broken down due to mechanical failures. Replacement parts for cars are very hard to get and, if available, are so expensive that most vehicles are kept running with home-made parts. It was heartwarming to see that the old East African custom of helping anyone overcome difficulties, had returned. Another notable fact was that as we neared Cuamba, the road improved visibly. We began to see villages surrounded by their cultivated fields, and roadside vegetable and fruit markets became more numerous.

At the Cuamba Campus I found a small collection of gems, picked up in the surrounding area and awaiting identification, and a group of thirty-four students of various ages, all eager to learn how to look for, recognize, and know the value of gems. It brought back pungent recollections of the courses that I used to teach at operating mines for African mine workers, when I was in charge of the Mines Development Service before independence.

The Campus is small; it only has a few classrooms and does not yet have any conventional laboratories. The aim of the University is to teach the returned refugees how to better use the land that was made available to them by the Mozambique government. The "Big Laboratory" is out there: in the undeveloped farms. And most of the time, that is where you will find the professors and the instructors.

I was given the use of a classroom twice a week, where I endeavored to teach the students how to identify minerals without using any of the usual scientific equipment. The only tools they had were any natural aptitude with which they had been born and the University's small gem collection, which I had classified. During the other days of the week, I traveled all over the areas that could be reached by car and visited operating mines—most of which consisted of a few holes dug in the ground with picks and shovels. I held impromptu classes for local prospectors, preferably under a mango tree because the sun gets very hot 14° south of the Equator. I classified and evaluated gems that were brought to me during these classes and wherever I stopped. At night I slept in African villages, where I was always received with kind hospitality and friendship.

During one of these trips, we passed through Metarica which is located about 14¼° south of the Equator, and 100 kilometers east of the northern tip of Lake Chilwa. I asked the driver to stop.

"There is nothing here," he replied. "No market, no shops, nothing to eat until we get to Marrupa."

"It is not that I am hungry, Micheias. I just want to walk down the street and take some pictures. My father built the first school north of the Lurio River here, in 1935."

On both sides of the only street of Metarica, the buildings have no doors, no windows, no roofs, and you do not see any people. But the street soon ends, and the houses inhabited by the Africans begin. The houses are surrounded by fences made of split bamboo, and huge mango trees grow inside the fences. It was worth traveling hundreds of miles, just to see those huge mango trees in flower!

People looked at this old white man with curiosity, but without resentment. The children waved at me and smiled. And I waved back at them, thinking of the gentle pioneer who could dream great dreams, and who had built the first schools for them. He would have agreed with me, "…*the people—like the grass after a wild fire—will always re-emerge with strength and vibrancy, to live like Africans and to be Africans.*"

Typical mountains of northern Mozambique, with one of the buildings of the Cuamba campus in the foreground. Photo by the author (July 2002).

Roadside vegetable market near Cuamba. In the foreground, manioc roots. In the middle distance from the left: pumpkins, guavas, a basket of kale leaves, and wild tomatoes (spread on a blanket). In the background at right, a plastic bucket filled with the ubiquitous green bananas. Photo by the author (July 2002).

Pegmatites bearing aquamarine and tourmaline gems radiate from granitic stocks similar to the one in the background of this photo. I am standing in a harvested field that has recently been reclaimed by returned refugees. Photo by the author (July 2002).

A group of returned refugees living in an African village near Cuamba are showing me their cotton crop. Photo by the author (July 2002).

Mango trees flowering in Metarica. The trees are covered with a profusion of sweetly scented white flowers. Photo by the author (July 2002).

Notes

1 The capital city of Mozambique was called Lourenço Marques under the Portuguese. The name was changed to Maputo after independence (1975).

2 My seven year commitment started from the time I received my Bachelor of Science degree in 1950. I stayed in the United States to complete my Master's degree with the permission of the Portuguese Government, and returned to complete the remaining six years with the Geological Survey.

3 Molócuè is pronounced mol-*oh*-qway; Gilé is pronounced *jeel*-ay.

The administrative divisions of Mozambique at this time were as follows. The entirety of Mozambique was administered by a Governor General. The country was divided into nine districts or provinces, each headed by a District Governor. The districts were subdivided into *circunscrições* (counties), lead by an *Administrador*. Each *circunscrição* was further subdivided into various *postos* (posts) which corresponded to the different African tribes in the area. Each *posto* was administered by a *chefe de posto* (chief of post), and each tribe was lead by its *muéne*, or chief.

The Monteminas concession covered a large area. About half of it was in the Alto Ligonha Post (corresponding to the Achirima people), and half was in the Gilé Post (corresponding to the Lomwe people). Alto Molócuè was the "county seat" for the *circunscrição* that included both of these posts.

4 Melela is pronounced meh-*leh*-lah; Lice is pronounced *leece*.

An "African road" is one of many trails connecting important places that have existed for centuries and are still in use by local African populations. Although very few outsiders know of them nowadays, they are very useful for reaching isolated places.

5 In northern Mozambique, a *makua* shower consisted of soaping yourself and then pouring water over your head with a tin can or the empty shell of a coconut (or in this case, an enamel cup).

6 A *panga* is a long bush knife.

7 The Achirima people manage to cook their meals over sets of three stones in almost any weather. When they go on long trips, they carry burning embers covered with ash inside a clay pot. The oldest person of the group is responsible for keeping the embers alive and starts the fires for the evening meal.

8 In the Zambezia District of Mozambique, the position of "car assistant" was a vital and important one, which required deep knowledge of local conditions and carried with it no small amount of prestige. The car assistant kept the car to which he belonged clean, kept the radiator full of water, the tank full of fuel, and air in the tires at the correct pressure. He knew the condition of all the roads in the area, maintained good social relations with the chiefs of the tribes, and talked them into repairing the bamboo bridges. Finally, he always knew where you could find game.

9 Three rifle shots fired in quick order is the traditional East African distress signal.

10 A pegmatite is defined as a coarse-grained igneous rock, found usually in dikes associated with large bodies of plutonic rocks. The name usually refers to granite pegmatites, although pegmatites with a mineral composition similar to the other plutonic rocks do exist. The granite pegmatites of Mozambique are world-famous for their richness in gems, tantalite and columbite minerals, and beryl.

11 In the Achirima language, *Muana* means "young man." This is the same term used in my own African name, *Muana Muano*, which means "Muano's Youngster." The story behind the name *Muana Muano* is told in the book *An African Name*.

12 Gasoline was sold in square tin cans, which were packed in specially-built wooden boxes, two tins to a box. Each tin carried four gallons.

13 Inselbergs are prominent steep-sided residual hills, that rise abruptly from the surrounding plains. The low lands surrounding them are surfaces of erosion that are generally true plains, as distinguished from peneplains.

14 The *capataz* is the leader, or foreman, of a group of workers.

15 For more about army ants, see *An African Name* (Chapter Twenty-six).

16 The Achirima people are a combination of many sub-groups, each governed by a triumvirate including the *muéne* (chief), a *samassoah*, and one or more *cabos*

de terras (literally, "land corporals"). Each *muéne* is the elected chief of a group; he owes obedience only to the Paramount Chief of the tribe, in this case my friend Novanana. Next down the chain of power are the *samassoahs*, appointed to their positions by the various *muénes*. At the head of the next lower echelon of the tribal government come the *cabos de terras*, also appointed by the *muéne* with the concurrence of the council of elders.

The council of elders is a consultative body made up of older and respected members of the nobility of the tribe. The council has a flexible function. They can interfere in any matter of interest to the tribe, from policy to politics, much in the same way the Roman senators did. Usually they advise and back the *muéne* in matters of justice and observance of the traditional laws and customs.

Distribution of land amongst the members of the tribe is supervised by the *cabos de terras* (singular: *cabo de terras*). Agricultural and other land is awarded according to its suitability for the needs of the applicant, but the tribe retains title to it. Occasionally, the right to use a plot of land may be passed onto female descendants upon the death of the person who was originally granted the rights. Eventually, however, the land is returned to the tribe. Men may not inherit land use rights, or own land. The *cabos de terras* also advise the *muéne* on matters related to the production, harvesting, and selling of crops, and may act in the capacity of sheriffs.

This system of government could be considered democratic, because the head of each group is their elected chief. However, the concept of *dimucracee* does not mean the same thing to Africans as democracy means to most of us, nor would their electoral system look very democratic to us.

When a *muéne* dies, resigns, or is impeached, the senior *samassoah* assumes the vacant position temporarily and starts looking for candidates whom he likes, to run for election. Usually the strongest candidate will be the oldest son of the oldest sister of the outgoing chief. This is because it is generally accepted that a man has the right to have a person of his own blood as his successor. It is also accepted that the sons of his oldest sister are for certain of his blood, while his own sons might not be.

Up to here, there remains some resemblance to a democratic way of succession, but things diverge further when you study the method of choosing the electors. Most of the voters are chosen from amongst people who have shown themselves to be friendly to the *samassoah's* candidate and to members of his family. They may also include anybody who owes him money or favors.

In practice, the system functions like the board of directors of the modern corporation. Each member of the board superintends in one specialized area, but decisions are taken by consensus and nobody sticks his nose in the area allotted to the other guy (not too much, anyway!).

17 Crazy beans, also known as buffalo beans, are the long velvet-covered seedpods of a wild creeper that is very common north of the Zambezi River. Skin contact with the fine hairs from the pods causes a fiery itch that may drive a person into fits, or even to temporary insanity. The antidote is provided by the wild custard-apple bush, which usually grows in the same areas as the beans. Rubbing the inner bark of the custard-apple bush over the affected areas relieves the itching and burning.

18 Pampuela is introduced in *An African Career* (Chapter Twelve).

19 *Havarra* is the Achirima word for "leopard."

20 *Shambas* are kitchen gardens: plots of land where Africans grow vegetables and fruits for personal consumption. The singular form is *mashamba*.

21 In mining jargon, the lower surface of an individual layer of rock is called the "footwall" of that layer. The upper surface, which again contacts the surrounding material, is called the "hanging wall."

22 I saw the Namivo Mine for the last time in 1975, long after I had left the company. While on a commercial flight from Nampula to Quelimane, I recognized the bright blue elliptically-shaped lake from the air. It was surrounded concentrically by cultivated fields. The mine superintendent's house seemed to have become a mission schoolhouse, and I could see sports fields around it. Everything looked tidy and peaceful.... I felt a pang of sadness because, in contrast, my beloved country was sliding inexorably into chaos and civil war. In fact, this trip was the last one I made to northern Mozambique in my position as mines inspector.

23 Much has been written criticizing the policies established by the Portuguese authorities in Mozambique, related to recruitment of African workers. As usual, some criticism was valid and some was tendentious and biased. Many authors were self-serving and envious of the good relations existing between whites and

blacks in the country. In too many cases, the writers were completely ignorant about the topic and should have checked their facts first.

Up until the time when the Portuguese fought against Ngungunhane, King of the Vátua and the last of the Zulu emperors, traffic of slaves was widespread in all the territories surrounding the Gaza Empire. The Gaza Empire was the name given to an extensive territory occupied by a loose congregation of African Nations and tribes of Nguni origin, which allied themselves under Ngungunhane's command to fight the Portuguese settlers in Mozambique. After Ngungunhane was defeated and exiled to the Azores (1896), the Portuguese government undertook a serious effort to organize the administration of its African territories. Laws were passed in Lisbon to protect the natives from being forced to work against their will. A more detailed account of the period and events that led to Ngungunhane's surrender is given in *An African Name* (Chapter Six).

Antonio Enes was the Royal Commissioner who conducted the wars leading to the destitution of Ngungunhane. Later, as Secretary for Colonial Affairs in Lisbon, Enes took the first steps towards building a legal structure to regulate recruitment of laborers in the Portuguese colonies. Under his direction, negotiations were conducted in 1897 between Mozambique and South Africa to develop new regulations for the recruitment and transportation of laborers to the South African gold mines.

In 1899, Enes wrote the Colonial Labor Law which introduced the concept of a two-level society. Under this system, the population of Mozambique was divided into "indigenous" and "non-indigenous" groups. The non-indigenous would be governed according to Portuguese Law and would have full Portuguese citizenship. The indigenous population would continue to follow the ancestral African laws, but would acquire some of the basic rights of a Portuguese citizen. Under the heading of "Ancestral African Laws" fell a varied collection of customs that included the right of the tribal chiefs to collect "taxes" in the form of uncompensated labor. This particular custom was known by different names in the many African languages of Mozambique, and in the Achirima language it was called *cassa-cassa* (sometimes pronounced *kwassa-kwassa*). Every healthy adult male had to give one week of free labor each year to his tribal chief. This labor was used to cultivate and harvest crops from the chiefs' fields and to build and repair local roads.

This custom was used "by extension" as a way for Africans to settle their annual tax debt to the Portuguese government, by doing work on the roads instead of paying the taxes in cash. When the concept was extended to the Portuguese government, the work was called *chibalo*, and the conscripted indigenous laborers, *chibalos*. The Portuguese *chefes de posto* thereby had authority to use *chibalos* to maintain public roads and bridges or, in case of war, as porters who followed the armies.

During the First World War, the German Army of Tanganyika invaded Mozambique, and intense fighting took place in the area that later became the Monteminas concession. The Anglo-Portuguese Army, under the command of General Jan Christian Smuts, met the invasion and eventually defeated the Germans. Thousands of *chibalos* belonging to the Lomwe and Achirima tribes were forced to follow the Allied Army, carrying on their heads the supplies, food, and ammunition needed by the troops. At the time that I was discovering mineral deposits and developing mines in the Monteminas concession, some of those *chibalos* were still living and gave me highly interesting descriptions of a war that historians have forgotten. (For more about the war, see Chapter Thirteen of *An African Career*.)

The Monteminas concession was outside the huge territory that was under the influence of the Witwatersrand Native Labour Association of South Africa. This organization still recruits every year hundreds of thousands of African men, to work in the mines of South Africa. Most of the workers are from southern Mozambique, Zimbabwe, Malawi, and Zambia. They contract to work in the mines for six consecutive months, after which they are sent home. After spending six months at home, they may be recruited again. They are not allowed to choose whom they want to work for, what kind of job they prefer to do, nor what salary they will be paid to do it. This system continues today with little change, and a large percentage of the foreign currency entering Mozambique is generated by these workers who are highly valued in South Africa.

24 Pontoons were very common all over East Africa in those days. They were wooden platforms built on top of empty oil barrels tied together with steel cables. The platforms were built long enough to carry one or more vehicles. Pontoons were usually powered by crews of several African "sailors," who propelled the contraptions by putting their weight on long bamboo poles that reached the river bottom. Usually the crew included a drummer, who beat a cadence followed by the pole wielders, and a "captain," who collected a fee for the service. The pontoons were sometimes tied by ropes and pulleys to a permanent steel cable that stretched from one bank of the river to the other.

25 The *cangarra* is a cylindrical container made of woven bamboo strips, usually about two meters long and one meter in diameter. People fill these containers with cotton or other produce and carry them to market, balanced on their heads.

26 *Rampahn* is the Achirima word for "bridge."

27 *Miricani* refers to the Americans.

28 *Mandioca* or manioc is a perennial woody shrub that produces an edible root also known as cassava. The roots are a staple food in many parts of Africa.

29 The bridge over the Melela River came to be known as the Morrua Bridge because it was close to Mount Morrua. The bridge was still in use as of 2004.

30 Tantalite is a mineral of the columbite-tantalite series. It is the principal source of tantalum, a valuable metal.

31 Achirimas and Lomwes were the main ethnic groups in the area of the concession. The Lomwe people occupied the western part, and the Achirima were settled in the central and eastern parts. The two tribes have similar customs and their languages have similarities, but neither trusts the other.

32 Mica is a mineral with perfect cleavage. Thin sheets of it separate easily, just like separating the pages of a book in parallel with a plane surface. In mica processing, skilled workers split "books" of mica into thin sheets by inserting a knife blade parallel to the perfect cleavage of the mineral. They manually remove inclusions of other minerals, discolored areas, and other defects, by cutting them out of the split sheets.

33 The Mocuba area, where Mugeba Post was located, was famous for its excellent deep blue aquamarine.

34 *Kaya*, or *cahia*, means "house." The term is also used for "home" and for "birthplace."

35 This story is told in *An African Career* (Chapter Twenty-five).

36 Adobe bricks are un-fired bricks made from a mixture of sandy soil with very little clay, averaging 18 inches by 9 inches by 8 inches in size. They are made by using thick wooden paddles to ram the almost-dry mixture into wooden molds.

37 Mozambique City occupies the whole surface of Mozambique Island (*Ilha de Moçambique*). The city was established long before the Portuguese navigator Vasco da Gama first stopped there in 1498. After Portugal claimed Mozambique, it became the colonial capital. Most of the original buildings were of adobe construction.

38 *Piri-piri* chicken (*frango piri-piri*) is a dish with Portuguese and African origins. Chicken is marinated in a hot chile pepper (*piri-piri*) marinade, and then grilled over the coals. Lemon or lime juice is often added to the marinade to help tenderize the meat and add a tangy flavor.

39 *Muhiua pama?* is "Did you hear?"

40 *Karramo* is the Achirima word for "lion" whether male or female. It is always capitalized in the written language.

41 The goatherd was referring to the electric generator.

42 **Brief Historical Background**
Many readers and acquaintances have asked me for an account of what led to the chaos, collapse of civil authority, terrorism, and guerilla warfare that preceded independence of the African colonies from Portugal. It is a complex subject connected with competing international economic interests. Those interests were vying for monopolistic control of oil fields and large diamond deposits on the west coast of Africa; for the then-unexploited fisheries of East Africa; and for the mineral wealth of central and southern Africa.

After the Second World War, there were several cases where new dictatorships were created by individuals who elevated themselves to the top by cynically riding on the innocent dreams of millions of starving people living in Africa and the East. The common people yearned for democracy and human rights, as promised by the intellectual liberalism that spread around the globe after the war. New leaders promoted themselves by promising to be the answer to those dreams, and once in power they maintained control by using the same kinds of massive propaganda techniques and political police forces that had brought the Nazis to power.

During the time that I write about, Portugal was a single-party dictatorship headed by Antonio Salazar, a professor of economics from one of the oldest and most respected universities in Europe. Salazar's rise to power had begun with a military coup d'état in 1926, that ended the First Republic. The military regime invited Salazar to serve as minister of finance, and he successfully brought Portugal out of a chaotic financial situation. He consolidated his power over the next several years, gaining the cooperation and admiration of the armed forces by equipping them with modern weapons and increasing their pay, and guaranteeing his popular acceptance through an alliance with the Catholic Church.

Portugal remained officially neutral throughout WWII, and at the end of the war Portugal's economic condition was sound. The country had become wealthy during the war by selling tungsten, tin, and tantalum ores to both sides of the conflict. The country had large gold reserves, and the low-priced raw materials coming from the colonies maintained the factories on a prosperous financial footing. Strong ties with the United States were in place, primarily due to a strategic military base in the Azores Islands which was leased by the Americans. There was little unemployment in the country, and some efforts to modernize industries were being started. If Salazar had stopped at this point and allowed the country to gradually become a democracy, following the footsteps of most of the other European countries, he would have become a respected and successful leader. However, dictators cannot stop. Instead of stepping down while still sailing in shallow waters, Salazar surrounded himself with even larger numbers of incompetent toadies. They would eventually help him sink the ship of state in deep waters.

Salazar's political party, *União Nacional* (National Union), became increasingly dominant and managed to win every election by suspiciously large majorities. A disorganized opposition, consisting of liberal intellectuals and monarchists, was easily controlled by PIDE (the political police). Opposition leaders were simply jailed whenever they managed to create a popular following. Opposition by the Communists was better organized and was supported by a strong underground organization. As a result, Communists were dealt with more harshly, by deportation to concentration camps in the Cape Verde Islands.

The post-war prosperity in Portugal was not shared by the Portuguese colonies. No serious efforts had been made to promote or assist their progress, and the colonies continued to be administered by a Ministry of Overseas that was staffed by arrogant, pompous and incompetent bureaucrats. The status of the colonies was firmly established: they were simply the suppliers of inexpensive raw materials that benefited a select group of financiers, who in turn monopolized the Portuguese industrial establishment.

Meanwhile, various European colonies in West Africa were in the process of becoming independent, and political movements and pressure groups were the fashion. Salazar's policies at home were extended into the colonies; in order to keep Mozambique isolated from outside influences, the political police became much more active and efficient at uncovering movements towards independence, and jailing their leaders. Newspapers and books were censored, and intellectuals who did not belong to the União Nacional were harassed. Every attempt was made to keep the population ignorant of any political trends that were occurring outside of Mozambique's borders.

However, due to the fact that hundreds of thousands of workers from Mozambique traveled every year to neighboring countries to work in mines (legally) and on plantations and in factories (illegally), news of the progress of the independence movements in Malawi, the Rhodesias, and South Africa filtered back into Mozambique. Furthermore, many black Mozambicans, while working outside the country, joined the movements that were then being born and the militant Marxist-controlled churches that were penetrating and grabbing power inside those movements. These circumstances gave rise to a situation where the rural Africans (who were supposedly illiterate, ignorant and uninterested in politics) were kept up-to-date about what was happening in the outside world. In contrast, the Europeans in Mozambique (who were mostly well-educated and lived in towns) were kept in the dark by a press strictly controlled by the central government's propaganda machine.

A curious phenomenon that occurred during this period, and which I have not seen mentioned by other writers, was the appearance of the "saucepan radios." These were short-wave radio receivers of good quality, housed inside war-surplus aluminum cooking pots. They were manufactured in the United Kingdom and sold at very low prices to the African populations in all the English-speaking territories that bordered Mozambique. In 1953–1954 while studying the geology of an extinct volcano in the Tete District of Mozambique, I had occasion to go to Zambia. (The Tete expedition is described in *An African Career*.) While I was there, I tried to buy a saucepan radio in a bush store. I was told that they were not for sale to white people. I did not argue with the storekeeper and left. At the next store that I saw near the road, I sent my cook inside and he came right out with a saucepan radio. I used it to listen to a variety of broadcasts: good music from Rhodesia; long-winded, self-promoting speeches from President Kaunda of Zambia; and incendiary Communist propaganda from Tanzania, which was loaded with hatred.

The pro-independence parties created in various territories around Mozambique started as disorganized groups led by intellectuals and idealists who craved power. For example, in the late 1950s UDENAMO (*União Democrática Nacional de Moçambique*) was founded in Bulawayo; UNAMI (*União Africana de Moçambique Independente*) in Malawi; and MANU (*União Nacional Africana de Moçambique*) amongst Mozambican immigrants of the Maconde Tribe in Kenya and Tanzania. At first, the new parties had little political power and no financing. However, in a very short time they were penetrated by activists trained in Algeria, and were protected, financed, and coddled by leaders whose countries had just become independent: for example, Kwame Nkhrumah of Ghana and Julius Nyerere of Tanzania.

Initially, the new movements did nothing but bicker and fight amongst themselves in characteristic tribal rivalry. However by 1964, under pressure from Nkhrumah and Nyerere, they coalesced into one large party named *"Frente Nacional para a Libertação de Moçambique,"* and called FRELIMO for short. Once FRELIMO was established, the saucepan radios took on a new role. They had initially been a powerful device for spreading Marxist propaganda amongst the African population; once guerrilla warfare was initiated by FRELIMO, the radios became a means of communicating with their isolated terrorist groups.

An American citizen of Mozambican origin, Dr. Eduardo Mondlane, became the leader of FRELIMO. Born in the Gaza District of Mozambique, Mondlane was educated in a Swiss mission in Mozambique and later attended the Witwatersrand University in South Africa. He was expelled from the University under apartheid regulations, and then went to the University of Lisbon. From there he traveled to the United States, studied at various universities, and eventually obtained his Ph.D. at Northwestern University.

Mondlane started his "career" with FRELIMO by ordering an attack on a small settlement named Chai, located south of the Mozambique-Tanzania border. Chai was the headquarters of a cotton-growing company which maintained a small police force, a hospital, and a few trading stores. When it was attacked by surprise, the local police—who were armed only with First World War rifles—put up a fight, but they were wiped out by the well-armed and well-trained attackers. Chai was completely destroyed, and all the population was massacred.

Timeline of important historical events
Ghana, 1958: The first meeting of representatives from eight independent African countries. The foundations of the independence movements were estab-

lished. Many future leaders of West African states, that eventually became independent, were present.

West Africa, 1958: Creation of the West African Federation of former French colonies. Independence of Guinea Conakry.

Lisbon, 1959: Portugal creates special anti-guerrilla military units.

New York, 1959: The General Assembly of the United Nations approves a resolution forcing Portugal to grant independence to its colonies. Appoints a commission made up of the United States of America, Great Britain, Holland, Mexico, Morocco, and India, charged with implementing the decision.

Cape Town, 1960: British Prime Minister Harold Macmillan makes a speech in defense of a "National African Conscience" and of the "wind of change." This is followed by a rash of more colonial independences.

Luanda, 1960: Creation of the "Movement for the Liberation of the Enclave of Cabinda."

Mueda (northern Mozambique), 1960: During a routine visit by the local governor, a crowd attacks the visitors without provocation. The governor's military escort arrives late and fires on the crowd, resulting in heavy loss of lives. The incident creates profound disaffection with the Portuguese amongst the Maconde tribe, one of the most important tribes in northern Mozambique.

Portugal, 1961: Failed *coup d'état*, led by influential military officers and aimed at forcing Salazar to make his African policies more democratic. Failure of this action effectively strengthened the opposing military leader, who wanted to conduct open warfare against pro-independence movements.

Chai, Mozambique, 1964: First terrorist attack by FRELIMO, under the leadership of Dr. Eduardo Mondlane.

Lisbon, 1974: Portugal's government is overthrown by a Marxist coup.

Mozambique, 1975: Under the terms of an agreement signed in 1974 between the new Portuguese government and FRELIMO, full independence was granted to Mozambique on June 24th, 1975.

Rhodesia, 1977: Formation of an anti-communist rebel movement called *Resistencia Nacional de Moçambique* (RENAMO).

Mozambique, 1977–1992: Civil war.

Rome, 1992: Peace agreement signed, ending the conflict.

[43] The *Front National de Libération de l'Angola* (FNLA) was started by Holden Roberto, an unsavory character who was backed by the United States State Department and the United Council of Churches, based in Switzerland.

[44] This story is told in *An African Career* (Chapter Six).

45 Lake Malawi is still shown on some maps by its former name of Lake Nyassa.

46 The colonial capital of Mozambique was on Mozambique Island, which is now part of Nampula Province. In 1907, the capital was officially moved south to Lourenço Marques, which was founded in the late 1700s and named for an early Portuguese trader. Nevertheless Mozambique Island remained the important government center in the north, and the provincial seat.

In 1935, the provincial seat was suddenly relocated to the town of Nampula on the whim of a Secretary of Colonies of the Portuguese Government. This move was related to the opening of the railway to Nampula. The story of our family's move to Nampula in those days is told in *An African Name* (Chapter Nine).

0-595-34005-9

Printed in the United States
77085LV00006B/36

9 780595 340057